Off to School

A Parent's-Eye View of the Kindergarten Year

Irene Hannigan

A 1998 NAEYC Comprehensive Membership Benefit

National Association for the Education of Young Children

Washington, D.C.

National Association for the Education of Young Children
1509 16ᵗʰ Street, NW
Washington, DC 20036-1426
202-232-8777 or 800-424-2460
Website: http://www.naeyc.org

Quotation on page 37: Reprinted with the permission of Simon & Schuster from *Zorba the Greek* by Nikos Kazantzakis. Copyright ©1953 by Nikos Kazantzakis.

Photos: cover & p. 29—Marietta Lynch; cover & p. 59—Hildegard Adler; cover & p. 77—Jean-Claude Lejeune; p. 105—Tim Johnson, the Photo/Image Library; schoolbus on cover and all other photos courtesy of the author.

Through its publications program the National Association for the Education of Young Children (NAEYC) attempts to provide a forum for discussion of major issues and ideas in the early childhood field with the hope of provoking thought and promoting professional growth. The views expressed or implied are not necessarily those of the Association. NAEYC wishes to thank the author, who donated much time and effort to develop this book as a contribution to our profession.

Library of Congress Catalog Card Number: 98-85536
ISBN: 0-935989-86-2
NAEYC #339

Cover design: Sandi Collins; *copyediting:* Catherine Cauman.

Printed in the United States of America.

For Ted

Contents

Preface

Ihave always enjoyed keeping a journal, so when my son Ted began kindergarten, it was natural that I would write many journal entries recording my reactions to my child's entry into the world of school. What I was not prepared for was how often and how much I would write.

During the course of my son's kindergarten year, I filled three five-by-eight-inch notebooks. My journal entries took the form of letters to Ted—letters that were never intended to be sent. I found myself squeezing in writing time whenever I could in those first weeks of school. Later, as routines were established, my entries too developed a predictable rhythm—although hardly a predictable pattern in terms of content. Sometimes I wrote a page, sometimes two or three, depending upon where my pen took me.

At the same time, Ted's teacher Ms. Yardley initiated a more public correspondence that, much to my pleasure and delight, came home every Friday in Ted's backpack. Her weekly messages to parents were at least two pages in length and covered every day of the school year. They were dedicated to "all the families and friends who ask their kindergartners, 'What happened at school today?' and get 'Nothing' for a reply!"

Clearly the focus and purpose of our reflections were different. My journal helped me savor the joys as well as grapple with the anxieties accompanying Ted's entry into public school. My feelings were very different from those I experienced when Ted began attending a child care program at age

16 months. As a new mother I had been preoccupied with my own anxieties about returning to work and the challenge of balancing my dual role of parent and working mother. My husband and I had chosen a child care program that provided open and informal lines of communication to help ease the transition. The fact that I was a teacher was of little relevance.

Now, however, as a teacher myself, my challenge was how to be the parent of a child in another teacher's class—how to understand another teacher's approach, have confidence in her, and get comfortable in my role as the parent of a school-age child.

As it turned out, Ms. Yardley's messages provided more than just answers to "what happened at school today." Strategically placed passages informed parents about her goals, what she valued, what was important, and how the year was progressing. I eagerly looked forward to them on Friday afternoons and read each and every word. She became someone I trusted and admired, and she also became someone who educated me. In fact, as the year progressed I found myself writing letters to her in my journal! In these letters Ms. Yardley was my confidante, my mentor, my friend.

This volume is a collection of selected letters—my journal entries and Ms. Yardley's messages to parents—juxtaposed to reveal the insights I gained during the course of the school year. Now my son is preparing for another school year—another transition lies ahead. But I find myself thinking I might already have learned "everything I ever needed to know" about being the parent of a school-age child during Ted's year in Ms. Yardley's kindergarten.

—Irene Hannigan

Acknowledgments

Numerous people provided me with feedback and support as I worked on this book. My husband Bob, whose opinion I value and trust, was convinced from the outset that this project was worth pursuing. He read my drafts, offered his opinions, and encouraged me throughout.

Karen Faler, Betsy Friedberg, Lois Licht, and Jim O'Brien are good friends who know both Ted and me. They offered sound suggestions on early drafts and also helped assuage my worries regarding Ted's reaction to so public a portrayal of his kindergarten year.

Karen Donahue, Susan Eckel, Christine Francis, and Betsy Warren-White, my colleagues in the Concord Public Schools, were generous in their insights both as educators and as parents. Their comments greatly helped me to focus my revisions.

Kathy Abba, Tom Dublin, and Mary Leonhardt gave me advice about publishers, and my mother Christine Leodakis gave me the confidence that I would indeed find a suitable publisher.

Carol Copple, my editor at NAEYC, has been wonderful in gently and respectfully guiding me through the publication process. I am also grateful for the care with which Tegan Culler and Catherine Cauman have edited my manuscript.

Finally I want to thank Mary Yardley, who appreciated the intent of my project from the beginning and graciously agreed to let me use her words along with my own.

—*Irene Hannigan*

Beginnings

1

Although school officially begins in September, by August most teachers start thinking about their classrooms and wondering about the children who will inhabit them. This August, however, my mind was not on Alcott School where I am the language arts curriculum specialist. Rather, my thoughts were on Bowman, the school where my son Ted would soon enter kindergarten.

We had just moved into the neighborhood, and apart from a positive experience at kindergarten registration and encouraging comments from neighbors, I had little knowledge of Bowman School. I only hoped Ted would be as comfortable there as he had been at his child care center.

On August 12 Ted received a letter in the mail. The return address was Bowman School, and I knew from the little bear stamp in the lower left-hand corner that the letter was from Ms. Yardley, his kindergarten teacher. Even though Ted loves to get mail, I greeted the letter with considerably more enthusiasm than he did. After all, for Ted Ms. Yardley and Bowman

School were just names, kindergarten was not yet a reality, and besides it was still summer!

Dear Ted,

I hope you are having a good summer. I am very glad that you will be in our kindergarten class this year. I love working with kindergartners, and I am really looking forward to working with you. I am sure we will have a good year together.

I have a favor to ask you. Will you please bring a recent photograph of yourself to school on the first day? I want you to tell your classmates and me about it, and then I will hang it up on our bulletin board. Thank you!

I will be working at Bowman in our classroom on Thursday, September 2, from ten o'clock till noon. If you can stop by, I would love to see you.

Love,

Mary Yardley

When my husband Bob read the letter to Ted, I was aware of the different reactions we each had. I could tell that Bob was mentally recording the task to be done before September and preparing to discuss with Ted the possibility that we would not be able to visit Ms. Yardley because we would be away on vacation. Ted asked why he had to take a photograph to school and announced in his quiet way that he didn't really want to. I loved the idea of a personal note to Ted from his teacher. Ms. Yardley's letter had an upbeat, reassuring tone, and it clearly communicated what seemed to me a reasonable request—a favor as she put it. Her letter also gave parents and children both a preview of one of the events that would occur on the first day of school.

While Ted may not have wanted to think about the specifics of kindergarten in mid-August, I welcomed this initial communication. It gave me reason to believe that some of my hopes and dreams for Ted's kindergarten year would be realized through Ms. Yardley, a teacher who made an effort to connect with children and their families even before the beginning of school.

A strong sense of connection and good communication were the hallmarks of the high-quality child care program Ted had attended. The daily routine of picking up Ted, chatting with his teachers, and reading the daily parent letter had kept me informed about some of the experiences he had had during his day. Thus I had become comfortable with the knowledge that Ted had a life away from home.

I was deeply interested in Ted's other life, and I hoped that he would share a little of it with me when he entered kindergarten. I anticipated that the level of communication and contact with his teachers that I had enjoyed in the past might very well drop, and that, along with the momentousness of Ted's entry into the world of public schools, brought on some pangs of nostalgia as September approached.

Dear Ted,

 This is a day I'll always remember: your first day of school. I was proud of you and, surprisingly enough, I was not as nervous as I had predicted.

 Much to your dismay—and to my great relief—there is no school bus service on opening day. As we headed toward the car, though, you swung your lunch box over your shoulder, turned to me, and said jokingly, "I'm going on the bus now," and you started across the lawn. I hope you'll be as eager to take the bus tomorrow.

 We arrived on time and found your classroom. You were some-what reserved with your teacher Ms. Yardley, and she didn't pressure you. Eventually you found your name tag among the assortment on a table and hung it on the pegboard. You would not hold on to the photograph of yourself that Ms. Yardley had asked you to bring, so I tucked it in your cubby. I didn't stay long, and we said good-bye without a fuss. I didn't cry. I guess I've done enough crying in private the last few days.

 When I picked you up from the extended-day program at four o'clock, you were in no rush to leave. You insisted on showing me

I still don't know
what you did
today. What
I do know is that
you came home
happy.

where the gym and cafeteria were, and I must say I am impressed that you could find your way around the school so easily. You seemed so proud to show me your school, and I welcomed the guided tour because I am curious about Bowman too.

I still don't know what you did today. You brought home a paper—now hanging on the refrigerator—that says, "My name is Ted. I am in kindergarten." What I do know is that you came home happy.

While you were playing before dinner, I felt compelled for some reason to make a batch of oatmeal cookies. Maybe I wanted you to have a pleasant smell to associate with your first day of school. Maybe I had guilt feelings because I'm not an at-home mom who stocks the cookie jar every day with homemade goodies to pack in your lunch. I'm not quite sure. I do know that there will be oatmeal cookies in your lunch tomorrow and you'll be taking the bus.

Love,

Mom

Thursday, September 9

Dear Ted,

    Today you rode the school bus for the first time. How excited and happy I am for you! Daddy unobtrusively took a picture of you climbing aboard Bus #4 and another one as the bus made its way down Carville Avenue. I would have felt foolish shedding a tear while you and your friends enthusiastically greeted the school bus.

    At the bus stop I learned that I wasn't the only parent whose child had awakened half an hour early in anticipation of the bus ride.

    You didn't tell me much about your day apart from describing the bus ride; but that's the way you tend to be. At your child care center, I always stopped to read the daily letter that highlighted the important activities of the day, so I had some understanding of how you spent your time. It will be different this year not having that kind of communication.

    Tomorrow you'll be coming home on the bus again, and I'll meet you. The bus driver's name is Donna. Parents at the bus stop seem to like her, and that's reassuring.

Love ,

Mom

Friday, September 10

Dear Ted,

    This morning as we ate breakfast you burst into song:

> *I hate you,*
> *You hate me,*
> *We're an angry family . . .*

Where did you pick up that song? When I asked, you casually replied, "Oh, some kids were singing it on the bus. Isn't it funny?"
    I could feel my stomach churning. Fortunately, before I could think of an appropriate response, you turned your attention to breakfast, the song forgotten. I wonder what choice lyrics you'll come home with next week.

Love,

Mom

Week one of school was now officially over, and Ted had made the initial transition. Had I handled things "right"? Knowing Ted, I did not insist that he wear a brand-new outfit the first day but let him wear clothes that were comfortable and familiar. Ted chose to carry our family backpack to school. Perhaps he considered it a milestone to be big enough to wear it himself and take care of it.

I was relieved and happy about the course of the first week. All eyes had remained dry, the bus ride was a huge success, Ted was happy, and there were even homemade cookies in the cookie jar. On Friday afternoon there was an unexpected bonus. When I checked through Ted's backpack, I came upon a three-page newsletter that seemed to address me personally:

This weekly newsletter is dedicated to all the families and friends who ask their kindergart-ners, "What happened at school today?" and get "Nothing" for a reply! Although it does not include everything in our day, it will give you a taste of what goes on.

Each entry begins with the date and number of days we have been in school. Part of our daily activities includes tracking and recording a variety of information, including the number of days we have been in school. These activities give children natural opportunities to develop skills such as data collection, record keeping, and pattern observation. Activities throughout our mornings are carefully chosen to help children continue to develop their mathematics and literacy skills through meaningful tasks.

What a pleasant surprise to receive this communication from Ted's teacher. Ms. Yardley voiced enthusiasm and optimism about how well the school year had begun. Entries for days one and two briefly described the Morning Song, which the children had learned using words and sign language, and how they had shared their photographs of themselves from home, drawn pictures, learned one another's names, and explored the classroom. Ms. Yardley transcribed the lyrics of the Morning Song—the first of many songs and poems to be sent home throughout the year for us to enjoy with Ted.

Among other items of interest, Ms. Yardley's first newsletter had answered my questions about enrolling in the milk program, when "specials"—music, art, library, and physical education— would be held, and whether children who rode the school bus would have time to play outside in the morning. I could hardly believe that this gold mine of information would be coming each and every week. I just hoped it would continue long enough to help me make the transition to school.

My name is

TED
_____

I am in

Kindergarten!

Monday, September 13

Dear Ted,

When I picked you up at school today, you again wanted to show me around. We saw the kinergarden classrooms where your buddies Sean and Patrick go. Outside you showed me the big circle on the blacktop where the kindergartners line up before school in the morning. Already you know so much about the school.

You talked a lot about the custodians who "own all the classrooms." How perceptive! I tried to explain that they really don't own the classrooms, but it does seem that custodians have a great influence on how smoothly schools operate. At my school they get to know the children quite well—perhaps because of all the balls they retrieve from the roof and the other problems they take care of. I don't doubt that the custodians play an important role at Bowman too.

Ms. Yardley's first weekly newsletter gave us an opportunity to talk a little about what went on in your classroom. With some prompting from your dad and me, you sang the Morning Song for us at dinner tonight (complete with signing). Would you ever have told us about this song on your own?

Love,

Mom

Tuesday, September 14

Dear Ted,

I picked you up at the bus stop today. How tall and responsible and independent you looked stepping off the bus! We still walk home hand-in-hand, but I wonder how long that will last.

I checked your lunch box to see what you'd eaten and what's left over. Today you said you didn't have time for the yogurt, cookie, and juice, but you ate your apple and the peanut-butter-and-jelly sandwich. Is lunch such a rushed affair?

Before bed tonight you talked more about school. "How many days have I gone to kindergarten?" you asked. I gather you're putting a penny in a jar for each day of school.

You loved the photographs Daddy took of you riding the school bus. I loved them too. When I came upstairs to tuck you in, I found you sitting cross-legged on the bed with the pictures spread out on the pillow. What were you thinking about?

Love,

Mom

Wednesday, September 15

Dear Ted,

   Today was library day. You got to pick out your own book, and you selected Eve Bunting's The Man Who Could Call Down Owls. *We read it together twice because you weren't quite sure what it was all about. We studied the detailed black-and-white line drawings. We made some predictions about the story based on our observations about the cover. You're usually hesitant to engage in this type of wondering (or at least to offer answers), but this time you offered some suggestions.*

   Later you said, "I'm learning to read because Ms. Yardley had a book that everyone read from." I wonder if you will learn to read this year. In my opinion there's certainly no rush.

   I look forward to your next library day. You'll probably bring home a book that's completely new to me, and I'll enjoy exploring it with you. What other new experiences will we share this year?

Love,

Mom

Right on schedule at the end of week two, another letter to parents arrived in the bottom of Ted's backpack. The newsletters included an entry for every day of school, and this one was chockfull of information. I learned about the importance Ms. Yardley places on shared reading, when the class enjoys reading Big Books together, and I gained a better understanding of what constitutes Worktime in her kindergarten. Her communication answered my questions about what reading looks like in kindergarten. Now I better understood Ted's comments when we read his first library book of the school year.

School Day #4
Monday, September 13

Today we read the Big Book *The Hungry Caterpillar* by Eric Carle. Big Books—oversize books with enlarged print—are an integral part of our reading curriculum in kindergarten.

Learning to be an effective reader is a process that begins before children even enter school. While most children do not learn to read independently in the kindergarten year, they do learn a great deal about reading that will help them to be effective readers later on. Big Books are wonderful tools for learning about the process of reading. After reading *The Hungry Caterpillar* (and discovering a mistake in it—butterflies hatch from chrysalises, not cocoons!), we made our own adaptation of the book. Once it is bound we will circulate it so that your children can share their innovative work with you.

School Day #5
Tuesday, September 14

Most days we have Worktime. This is a time when there are many activities and centers open to the children, and they are able to decide where they want to work. Sometimes there are activities that all the children must do. We call these Red Star activities. At the beginning of the year we have few required tasks. The emphasis for the children is on learning about what's available in the room, getting to know each other, and learning routines.

At the beginning of each Worktime, I put a list of activities on chart paper. Children tell me where they want to begin. They always have the option of suggesting their own activities, allowing them to pursue what interests them. The Pretend Center and Block Corner have been very popular, and I am pleased to see both boys and girls in each area. There have already been some cooperative efforts on block structures that I have never seen before. We really have a very creative group.

While as a teacher I am quite well versed in the theoretical underpinnings of a more comprehensive approach to reading instruction, I could feel myself as a parent having a difficult time applying that knowledge at home. I worried that I would be too heavy-handed with Ted, wanting to do too much explicit teaching before he was ready. It also occurred to me that because my formal teaching experience has been in the primary grades,

I did not have firsthand knowledge of how kindergarten children emerge as readers. I worried that I would apply unrealistic standards to Ted's progress. I therefore regarded the information that Ms. Yardley provided as a great support in my own learning. Whether or not I would be able to apply that new knowledge in my interactions with my own child was another matter.

I was reminded of the many parents of kindergartners and first-graders at Alcott School who seek guidance about how best to support their child's initial efforts in reading. Suddenly I had a much deeper appreciation of the challenges facing the parent of a school-age child. I couldn't help but feel guilty. As an educator was I doing enough in my own school community to help parents understand the supportive role they play in their child's literacy development? I considered Ms. Yardley's messages one of the best examples of teacher communication I'd seen.

I also found myself picking up on the offhand comments that would become a pattern in Ms. Yardley's newsletters. Many had to do with the creativity of the children and her respect for their individual abilities and personalities. Her honest, genuine praise of children's work would continue to come through in these comments throughout the school year.

Learning about each child was Ms. Yardley's stated priority during the beginning of the school year, and she invited parents to write a note to her with any thoughts we might have about our children. She also understood the hesitation of those parents who might prefer that she become acquainted with the child in this new environment without their preconceptions.

Ms. Yardley had a wonderful ability to make her communications come to life, as she did in the Wednesday, September 15, entry. The newsletter at the end of the first full week of school continued to inform parents about the process of reading.

School Day #6
Wednesday, September 15

Today we sang two songs about caterpillars and butterflies. The songs are written out on a large piece of oaktag. As we sing together, I point to the words. While the children enjoy the song, they learn to match the words they are singing to the words on the page, and they learn that we read from left to right and from top to bottom on a page. These are important skills for children.

Your children already know a great deal about the process of reading. Today, as I introduced a new song, I stopped when we got to a word that began with *b*. I puzzled over it and asked them, "What do you think that word might be?"

Many shouted out, "Butterfly!"

Astonished, I asked, "How did you know that?"

The children said, "I saw the *b*" and "It rhymes with *my* from the line before."

I said, "*Bananas* starts with *b;* why didn't you guess bananas?"

The children shouted, "That doesn't make sense!"

They are already using effective strategies, attending to context and letter sounds to figure out new words. What an enthusiastic group we have.

Creating a classroom environment that "makes sense" was clearly Ms. Yardley's agenda from day one. A study of insects would be the focus during the initial weeks of school. The songs, poems, and books to which she introduced the children enhanced the study of their classroom "pets"—a giant Madagascar cockroach and a caterpillar.

Wednesday, September 22

Dear Ted,

Ms. Yardley's weekly communications are invaluable. I now have contexts that help me understand some of your comments pertaining to school activities.

You're talking a lot more about school these days. I can never predict when these discussions will take place. You've been singing a lot too. You've been watching a caterpillar that will eventually become a monarch butterfly—how exciting! You've been reading Eric Carle's The Hungry Caterpillar, *and today you showed me your Class Book based on the story. You knew exactly which page in the book was yours. These are just the sorts of activities I'd hoped your kindergarten teacher would offer, and I think I enjoy hearing about them almost as much as you enjoy doing them.*

Your photograph from home is still not posted on the wall outside your classroom. You said you wouldn't share it; I should have believed you. You told me, "It's too special to share." That sounds like something Ms. Yardley may have said to you. You finally must have felt comfortable about putting your self-portrait up, though. You're such a good artist.

This has been a hard week for me. I'm having trouble completing all my work at school, but I imagine I'll get better at handling everything.

Love,

Mom

I remember how I felt when I noticed that blank spot where Ted's photo should have hung on the bulletin board outside his classroom. There was a photograph of everyone else in addition to their self-portrait and name tag. I fought the urge to jump to conclusions about why my son didn't want to share his photograph with the group. Did it mean he was resisting other activities? Would it become a pattern?

How easily I could have drawn all sorts of inappropriate conclusions. Instead I forced myself to see the bigger picture: Ted's self-portrait was hanging proudly, and the smile in that picture was the smile I had seen each day so far this school year. I decided that the missing photograph was an issue between Ted and Ms. Yardley; I should stay out of it.

The information in Ms. Yardley's next two newsletters rounded out the first phase of communication about what she wanted parents to know about her teaching. Learning about Meeting reinforced the priority she gave to purposeful activities that help children make meaning. Learning more about what forms reading takes in a kindergarten class further enriched my understanding of the process.

School Day #8
Friday, September 17

In our class we start each day with a class meeting. During Meeting we do a number of routine activities. The activities are listed on sentence strips on a hanging chart. Each strip has a word and a picture clue. After we do each activity, we remove the corresponding sentence strip from the chart. This design helps the children take an active part in following our agenda. You can be sure they quickly speak up if I forget to take off a strip, and they love to call out what's next. It won't be long before they will be running Meeting themselves. Won't that be great?

One activity we do each day is track the temperature. A thermometer hangs outside our back door. The thermometer is color coded to show ranges of temperatures. During Meeting, the person with the temperature job chooses a friend, and together they bring in the thermometer. We often make predictions about what range the temperature will be in. Once we learn what it is, we record the temperature color range with a square of matching color paper on a hanging chart. On this same chart we also record the number of days we have been in school. This record-keeping system affords many fun opportunities for math- and science-related questions.

School Day #9
Monday, September 20

We read Big Books every day. Sometimes we read books around a theme we are studying, such as *The Hungry Caterpillar*. Other times a book will catch someone's eye, and we read it simply because it looks good. Our classroom is a place where we encourage and treasure each other's enthusiasm for books.

The other day a child was very interested in reading *Greedy Cat* by Joy Crowley. After just one reading it became a class favorite, and today we made our own adaptation of *Greedy Cat*. It too will be circulating soon. I know you will enjoy it!

School Day #10
Tuesday, September 21

Today we read our second completed Class Book, an adaptation of *Greedy Cat*. The children take such pride in their work. One child said today as he gazed around the room, "Look at all the beautiful work we have done!"

Next we acted out the original story of *Greedy Cat*. We act out stories in our class. Not only is it enjoyable, but acting out stories necessitates that children truly understand what they have heard and then puts that knowledge to work. It was delightful to see the many different ways the children chose to reenact the story.

How valuable it was to have a teacher explain the context of classroom activities. When the children's version of *Greedy Cat* came home one day in a protective cloth bag, Ted's dad and I greeted it with due respect. We had heard about it from Ted, had seen the finished product at Back-to-School Night, and were eagerly anticipating its arrival.

Needless to say, not all of Ms. Yardley's communications were directed solely toward helping parents understand the theoretical underpinnings of her classroom. She also took great care to keep us informed about the progress of the caterpillars as well as the pure fun the children had picking apples. At times very different descriptions of the same activity appeared in my journal entry and Ms. Yardley's letter.

School Day #16
Wednesday, September 29

What fun we had today! With the four other kindergarten classes and many helpful parents we went apple picking at an orchard in Stow. We had beautiful weather and picked lots of delicious apples. After picking, we had a snack in the field and arrived back at school at the end of the morning. Many, many thanks to all who chaperoned. We appreciated your help and enjoyed your company!

Wednesday, September 29

Dear Ted,

Today was apple-picking day; you were exhausted when you got home. I expected to see more than the five small apples and one brownish, half-eaten one in the bottom of your shopping bag. "The other apples rolled out," you explained. You seemed pleased with the five you brought home and decided to polish them. "This apple juice tastes like cider," you commented; you didn't say much else about the trip.

I hope you'll like the apple crisp your class is making tomorrow.

Love,

Mom

So ended September of Ted's first year in public school. In 15 days I had learned a lot about the kind of classroom in which my son would be spending his time. Some of the information came from Ted, some from Ms. Yardley, and some from my own pen as I became committed to using my journal to make meaning of the snippets of information that came my way. It occurred to me that perhaps Ted was doing the same, in his own way, as

Her parent letters
were an impor-
tant communica-
tion tool. They
enabled parents
to trust not only
her professional
expertise but also
her personal
commitment to
nurturing and
supporting the
capabilities of
each child.

a new member of a school community. This was reassuring to me in my new role as a parent of a school-age child.

I thought back to the days when I'd had a classroom of my own, and I wondered how my perceptions as a teacher may have differed from those of my students and their parents. I was struck by the enormous challenge a teacher has even to begin to understand the impact of her work on the lives of the children who make up her complex and varied classroom community.

I found myself regarding all school-age children, including my son, with deep admiration. I realized the breadth of their ability to adjust to new situations, to accept new expectations and routines, and to work hard at understanding and making sense of their new environment in their own way. Admittedly some children may have an easier task than others because they are in particularly effective schools with excellent teachers and supportive home environments. Yet there is still a profound need for the adults in children's lives to nurture this inclination.

Ms. Yardley's way of responding to that need was to create a purposeful classroom grounded in developmentally appropriate practice. Her parent letters were an important communication tool. They enabled parents to trust not only her professional expertise but also her personal commitment to nurturing, respecting, and supporting the particular talents and capabilities of each child.

My own response, I was beginning to see, was to grow more confident in my son's ability to assume responsibility and control over his school life. I needed to come to terms with the fact that, while I might always be more knowledgeable about school in general, Ted would become the expert about his school in particular. I wouldn't always know what was best. I couldn't always fix things for him. As time went on it would increasingly become his responsibility to understand and negotiate his school world, to become engaged in learning, and to work hard.

Fall

eyond Ms. Yardley's weekly communications, the school newsletters, and the miscellaneous flyers that found their way into his backpack, Ted brought home few papers, art projects, or drawings to hint at how he spent his time in kindergarten. He occasionally spoke of his paintings and drawings hanging on the classroom walls or of Class Books in the works, but very little individual work came home during the first six weeks of school.

This was in contrast to Ted's extended-day experience, from which he brought home projects and worksheets and papers that more typically characterize the kindergarten programs I had been most familiar with. Each day it seemed Ted brought home something he had done at extended day, and these products helped us keep abreast of the extended-day program. While I was impressed with the time and energy the teachers clearly gave to the program and felt very lucky indeed to have child care available within Bowman School, I did perceive the two portions of the day as very separate—

one was kindergarten and one was not—and I think Ted too saw them as quite distinct.

When Ted brought home an elaborate finished product that I could hardly believe was his—for example, a large, intricate color-by-number dinosaur picture—I usually checked with him to see whether he had done it with Ms. Yardley or at extended day; typically it was the latter. Yet I wasn't always comfortable about the rationale for having the children produce these pieces. If he brought home a paper or a worksheet, I first wanted to know whether he had enjoyed doing it and understood the point of it. I didn't say anything to Ted, but I worried that too many worksheets would set the expectation that school was about filling in worksheets.

Although Ted usually seemed pleased when his projects found a place on our refrigerator or in another prominent location in our house, I sometimes felt he distanced himself from his work from extended day, seeming to take little ownership of it. Though most of the work we displayed at home was done during the extended-day session, I was unwavering in my conviction that valuable work—the most important work, in fact—was going on in Ms. Yardley's kindergarten.

How did other parents interpret the lack of tangible products coming home from kindergarten every day? I wondered. In many of the more developmentally appropriate, process-oriented classrooms in my own school, the same situation exists. As teachers move toward more authentic portfolio assessment, it becomes critical for children's work to be saved over time rather than sent home regularly, never to be seen again.

Fortunately the daily accounts in Ms. Yardley's letters provided me with a good sense of the kind of learning my son was engaged in, and my observations confirmed her words. What if there had been no written communications? How would I have known?

School Day #25
Wednesday, October 13

We have an Art Center in our room. It holds a collection of beautiful junk: toilet paper rolls, meat trays, egg cartons, yarn, tissue paper, and construction paper as well as paper punches, scissors, tape, markers, and crayons. Everything is out and available to the children to use for building and creating. Children often work at the Art Center before our Meeting or during Worktime.

The emphasis in our Art Center is on process and the act of creating rather than on an end product. There is no right or wrong way to do an art project, and often the most learning takes place in the conversation and experimentation done around the table.

Today children made toys for their pets out of toilet paper rolls and toy pets out of egg cartons. How creative!

Wednesday, October 13

Dear Ted,

You've been paying a great deal of attention to letters and words this week. You spell words that are around you and ask what they say: C-E-N-T-E-R on the back center seat belt, E-X-I-T above the door at school, O-N, O-F-F, S-T-O-P, G-O.

You also seem more aware lately of the letters' sounds and how letters are shaped. You form them with your fingers and parts of your body. Have you been bending your body into letter shapes at school with Ms. Yardley? I'll bet some letters require two people!

I wonder if you're doing any writing in your class.

Love,

Mom

As soon as your child spends a significant amount of time away from home, you are struck by the reality that you can't possibly know all he is encountering during the course of his day. No longer the sole orchestrator of experiences, activities, and opportunities you think are worthwhile for your child, you have to face the fact that someone else is sharing the task of educating him. The parent is left trying to put together the puzzle pieces. Where did that comment come from? How did he know that? What prompted that question? While it's intriguing sometimes to do detective work, it's a great relief when the other orchestrator sheds some light on the subject.

Because Ted had attended a child care program since he was 16 months old, kindergarten was by no means my first experience in dealing with this reality. I remember how appreciative I was then of the wonderfully informative letters outlining the day's events that his teachers tacked to the parent bulletin board each morning. Those written communications along with the opportunity, when I picked Ted up, to chat informally with his teachers about his experiences were enormously useful in helping me understand his day. Because picking up Ted at kindergarten was not a possibility for me, Ms. Yardley's weekly communications served an especially important function.

School Day #28
Monday, October 18

Today we read the Big Book *Pumpkin, Pumpkin,* which tells the story of how a tiny seed grew into a giant round pumpkin. Then we each drew something we remembered from the story and wrote about it.

Writing is a complicated process, and I am so pleased with the hard work our kindergartners are doing. After they have drawn their pictures, they think about what they want to write. They say the words slowly and listen for the sounds in each word. Then they have to figure out which letters go with those sounds and *then* write those letters down. That's challenging!

By the time Back-to-School Night arrived in mid-October, I had formed my own impressions of what kindergarten in Ms. Yardley's classroom was all about. Ted was one source of information, Ms. Yardley's messages were another, and my own musings and reflections rounded out the picture. It seemed to me that a tremendous amount of learning had occurred for all of us during Ted's first 27 days of school, and Back-to-School Night was an important opportunity to hear directly from Ms. Yardley about her program.

Sitting on small chairs arranged in a circle, much the way our children did each day, we had Meeting with Ms. Yardley. She gave us a five-page handout outlining the evening's agenda. She discussed how the kindergarten curriculum is taught within the context of daily routines and activities, and she shared with us the children's daily schedules. Ms. Yardley then elaborated on some important activities she had planned for the year: Class Books, Writing Folders and Big Black Journals, Swimmy, third-grade Book Buddies, and Important Person.

We listened attentively as Ms. Yardley explained with honesty and enthusiasm her approach to kindergarten. She invited questions, but there were few. Everyone seemed to feel pleased and lucky that she was "our" teacher. Ms. Yardley passed out another page for us to read at our leisure. It was from *Zorba the Greek* by Nikos Kazantzakis:

I remembered one morning when I discovered a cocoon in the bark of a tree, just as a butterfly was making a hole in its case and preparing to come out. I waited a while, but it was too long appearing and I was impatient. I bent over it and breathed on it to warm it. I warmed it as quickly as I could and the miracle began to happen before my eyes, faster than life. The case opened, the butterfly started slowly crawling out and I shall never forget my horror when I saw how its wings were folded back and crumpled; the wretched butterfly tried with its whole trembling body to unfold them. Bending over it, I tried to help it with my breath. In vain. It needed to be hatched out patiently and the unfolding of the wings should be a gradual process in the sun. Now it was too late. My breath had forced the butterfly to appear, all crumpled, before its time. It struggled desperately and, a few seconds later, died in the palm of my hand.

That little body is, I do believe, the greatest weight I have on my conscience. For I realize today that it is a mortal sin to violate the great laws of nature. We should not hurry, we should not be impatient, but we should confidently obey the eternal rhythm.

I filed the page away in the binder where I kept Ms. Yardley's newsletters. I also saved the caption from a poster in the classroom that caught my eye. It read,

Childhood:
A journey not a race

Monday, October 18

Dear Ms. Yardley,

Back-to-School Night is your opportunity to give parents an education, and I don't know how to even begin to convey my appreciation and admiration for the thoughtful, purposeful, and caring classroom environment that you described to us tonight.

It took me a while to digest one of your opening statements: "Curriculum is taught through our daily routines and activities." I think you mean, for example, that Meeting can last 45 minutes if something worthwhile is happening; there's no mad rush to move on to the next activity.

Thank you for making Ted's introduction to public school an example of what learning can and should be in a school setting.

Ted's Mom

When I took my pen in hand late on that Monday evening in October, I was surprised to discover that I was addressing my journal entry to Ms. Yardley rather than to Ted. There were to be many more letters to Ms. Yardley during the next few months. By March I would have written almost as many letters to Ms. Yardley as to Ted. Only one was actually delivered to her.

Wednesday, October 20

Dear Ms. Yardley,

Ted and I have been working on a chapter book together called "Everyone Come and Have Some Fun." Tonight we finished it. Without missing a beat Ted calmly announced, "I'm taking this to school tomorrow. Let's put it in my backpack." He raised his eyebrows the way he does when he's particularly excited and said, "We'll read it at Meeting."

It's so exciting to see his knowledge of story come out in his writing. Each chapter is a story with a beginning, a middle, and an end. They all start out with "Once upon a time." He even created a table of contents.

It's the first time I've seen Ted want to share something of himself with you. I'm sure you'll know how to receive it.

Ted's Mom

P.S. I enjoyed seeing Ted's October self-portrait on the bulletin board outside the classroom door. I like your idea of having the children draw a self-portrait each month. By the way, I noticed that Ted has finally hung up his photograph. How did this come about?

Thursday, October 21

Dear Ms. Yardley,

This was a big literacy evening as well as Ted's dad's birthday. As I read the newspaper, Ted kept pointing out letters and numbers: T-H-E B-O-S-T-O-N G-L-O-B-E, O-C-T-O-B-E-R 2-1. Then under his breath he said, "Hey, this is the Year of the Rooster and Dad's birthday!"

We read The Hungry Caterpillar *together, and it was the first time Ted read along with me. Sometimes he lets me point to the words, but sometimes he very deliberately pushes my hand away. Then we read* It Looked Like Spilt Milk.

Bedtime reading is almost always done with his dad—lots of short stories from anthologies, which Ted seems to love. I'm sure that's one of the reasons he wanted to make his chapter book. (Ted told me you liked it.)

Ted's Mom

Friday, October 22

Dear Ms. Yardley,

 Numbers also are playing a big part in Ted's life lately. I couldn't follow everything he said tonight, but I caught, "eight plus two equals ten"—all in the course of avoiding his dinner. Ted reads the numbers on digital clocks and newspaper flyers. He read "62," "88," and "16" tonight. He tries to count to 100, and he also counts backward. Tonight he tried counting odd numbers to 11, then even numbers.

Ted's Mom

I'd read about periods of equilibrium or disequilibrium. This seemed to be a period of equilibrium for Ted. Compared with how he had been behaving a short time ago, he seemed much more settled and content. And he was showing an enormous burst of cognitive awareness and interest in letters and numbers.

School Day #33
Monday, October 25

What an exciting day! When we arrived this morning we found that one of our painted lady butterflies had emerged. Then during the morning three more emerged. One seemed to be having a hard time, floundering on its back; but when we put it on cotton balls soaked in sugar water, it seemed to recover. The butterflies can live happily in our cage for several days. We decided that Jack's birthday, which is Thursday, would be a good day to release them.

Ms. Yardley's entry reminded me of the excerpt from *Zorba the Greek* that she had distributed at Back-to-School Night. Rereading that passage, I thought about a child's development and the unbelievable challenge a teacher is handed when we entrust to her an entire class of very different little evolving beings. While 5-year-olds have certain common characteristics and predictable patterns of development, there are as many different biological clocks ticking as there are children in a classroom. There are many "ways of being," and this fact informed Ms. Yardley's way of being a kindergarten teacher.

Parents' knowledge of child development is limited by their fairly narrow frame of reference: the development of their own child. Those with more than one child may gain a broader perspective. A teacher, though, has the advantage of observing the growth and development of many children, and her perspective on child development is a wonderful resource for parents.

Predictably, periods of equilibrium are followed by periods of disequilibrium. While Ms. Yardley's newsletters for the beginning of November continued to be about new units of study and updates on ongoing activities, my letters focused on some upsets.

Wednesday, November 3

Dear Ted,

You got home a little later than usual tonight after going to Drumlin Farm with the extended-day program. You were tired, but you said something that really surprised me, and I'm not sure what to make of it. Because it's Wednesday—library day—I asked if you'd gotten a library book. You not only replied, "No," but you also went on to say that you really didn't like going to the school library or selecting books. Then you said, "I don't really like the whole place."

What's up? Do you mean it? It is true that you haven't come home with a book for two weeks. Should I talk to Ms. Yardley about your attitude toward the library?

Love,

Mom

Dear Ted,

You haven't been finishing your lunch lately. When I asked, "Am I giving you too much?" you launched into a discussion about not having enough time at lunch and how certain foods take

longer to eat: "Pudding and applesauce and yogurt are things I'll just eat at home from now on."

It's too bad that the rather civilized lunch routine you had at your child care program, where your teachers used to sit down and eat with you, is not possible in the typically chaotic atmosphere of a school cafeteria.

Love,

Mom

Wednesday, November 17

Dear Ted,

I knew it would happen sooner or later. Tonight you used my least favorite word in the English language. As you sprawled out on the couch after dinner you said, "Today was BORING." This came as a surprise since you had talked quite happily about the day on our way home from school.

I asked, "What does boring *mean?"*

After skirting the issue, what came out was that you really didn't want to go to extended day—that's what you had called boring. Instead you'd prefer to come home on the bus to a sitter. When I questioned you further, I learned that one of the boys with whom you'd developed a fast friendship at extended day was dropping out of the program. He'd explained to you that a sitter would come to his home to care for him while his parents were at work.

Dad came downstairs as we were talking. He pretty much closed the subject by explaining that it's hard to find a sitter and that there are good teachers to take care of you at extended day.

Love,

Mom

It is difficult
to know how
seriously to
consider a
particular
incident and
easy to magnify
what could be
an isolated or
minor concern.

Wednesday, November 17

Dear Ms. Yardley,

Ted brought home a library book this week—probably because you reminded him—but he's really not happy about it. He went on and on, sputtering about how you said it was his "work" to pick out a book and that he disagreed. Such vehemence! I can't figure out what the issue is. I'm tempted to drop you a note, but I fear I'll be making too much of it.

And one of Ted's extended-day teachers has been reporting for several days that "Ted misses his dad and feels sad about it." When I assured his teacher that Ted's father is not traveling and that they spend lots of time together, we agreed to find out what might be behind Ted's sadness. It turns out that one of Ted's new friends hasn't been at extended day for a while and Ted misses him.

I know I can't take every little crisis to heart, but right now I feel overwhelmed. I hope you'll tell me when there's an important issue to address.

Ted's Mom

The tone of November's entries, one after another, was worried, anything but mellow. Each of the issues that surfaced, while different in nature, touched me at a vulnerable point. I easily could have let any one of them cloud what had begun as a great school year. Maybe that was part of the problem. It's difficult for a parent to accept the fact that life for one's child cannot be perfect.

Throughout Ted's early years, Bob and I prided ourselves on our ability to anticipate problems and orchestrate situations to make life less stressful and more satisfying for our family. We weren't successful one hundred percent of the time, but when Ted was in our care for most of the day, we had more control over how the day went. We were better able to understand his outbursts or mood swings. We could account for the behavior changes that characterize any given day because we understood their context.

I remember during the child care years, after I had returned to work, how much I appreciated spending my school vacation times with Ted. I could then connect with his rhythm and temperament in a way that's next to impossible when you're apart. What I now realize, as the parent of a school-age child, is that the opportunity to be closely in sync with one's child greatly diminishes with each passing year. That is perhaps one of the reasons it is difficult to know how seriously to consider a particular incident and easy to magnify what could be an isolated or minor concern.

Fortunately, of the three incidents that came up in November, the one that bothered me most was easiest to remedy. When the word "boring" came out of Ted's mouth, I first thought he was saying that Ms.

Yardley's kindergarten was boring—that he didn't share my enthusiasm for the teacher I so admired. I was relieved when I realized he was referring to the extended-day program.

Bob and I could have succumbed to the pressure and feelings of guilt that children inflict on parents at times, but we didn't. We felt that the school's extended-day program provided the kind of supervision that would be beneficial to our son. It seemed to us that by midyear most children, having adjusted to the longer school day, gain a lot from making new friendships and participating in the activities offered at extended day. We believed Ted would too, and eventually we saw we had made a good decision.

The library issue was more problematic because it cut to the core of something I valued. I needed to sort through my thoughts about Ted's reaction. Did I really care if he brought home a book each week? He certainly had plenty of reading material without an additional selection from the school library. Was I worried that Ted was getting turned off to reading because he didn't like going to the library? I can't say there was any evidence of this; Ted always greeted the purchase of new books with great delight, and he never declined the chance to listen to a good story. Was I worried that Ted's obstinacy would earn him an unfavorable reputation with the librarian? I assumed the librarian or Ms. Yardley would contact me if they felt there was a problem.

It occurred to me that Ted might simply be overwhelmed at the prospect of choosing a book from the large selection at hand. Because he is accustomed to my guidance or has become dependent upon it during our visits to the public library, perhaps he needed to learn to select books on his own in this new setting. I began to think that it would do nothing but create problems if I were to force the issue.

The third concern—lunch in the cafeteria—was something I knew was beyond my control. I could only hope that Ted would be able to deal with the chaotic lunchroom environment. In fact, by altering some of his lunch box choices to suit the shorter lunch period, he indeed seemed to be adapting. I reminded myself to be supportive of Ted's mechanisms for coping with the situation himself rather than step in and handle the problem for him.

As anyone who has worked in one knows, schools are complex organisms. There are a multitude of competing priorities and problems, any one of which takes time and resources to deal with. Experience tells me that, in every effective school, principals and staff operate with a vision that informs and focuses their energies in any given school year. Parents need to understand the school's priorities, offer their input at an appropriate time and in an appropriate manner, and then be ready to pitch in and do some of the required work, however mundane it seems. I felt that since I couldn't help directly by volunteering in either the library or the cafeteria, I might do better to hold off on raising a concern. After all, the school staff had been very effective in getting things working more smoothly in many areas that had needed improvement. My concerns might well be on their list of problems to be addressed. I decided to find out more about the school's priorities and plans over the next few months.

> . . . you anticipated my questions, showed me examples of my son's work, spoke with knowledge and confidence about his transition to kindergarten; you made me feel Ted is in good hands.

Given the ups and downs of November coupled with the anticipation of the fast-approaching holidays, parent conferences couldn't have come at a better time, and Ms. Yardley didn't let me down.

Thursday, November 18

Dear Ms. Yardley,

Thank you for a good conference. You described to a tee the Ted I know and yet gave me new insights about him as a learner—as a kindergartner. The thing you said that I probably feel proudest about is that you believe Ted comes to school ready to learn and enthusiastic rather than bored. At home we've tried to offer him experiences and opportunities to grow and learn without "teaching" or pressuring him. I'm glad his attitude reflects that.

I was excited to hear about Ted's interest in Big Books. I understand your comments about his ability to make predictions and use cueing systems and strategies. Those are areas of performance I neither could nor would want to try to assess myself. We just read to him. However, we do point to words and will start getting him to think about doing that as well.

You said Ted has a good sense of story. I too was struck by this when we wrote that little book together. I'm sure it's directly attributable to the fairy tales and folktales Ted's dad reads to him at bedtime.

Our conference was informative. You anticipated my questions; you showed me examples of my son's work; you spoke with knowledge, enthusiasm, and confidence about Ted's transition to kindergarten; and you made me feel that Ted is in good hands.

Thank you, Ms. Yardley.

Ted's Mom

Just as I was congratulating myself on making the right decisions about the issues that had surfaced in November, I fell back into the difficulty of creating a problem for Ted and myself one Monday morning in December at breakfast. The situation was a bit like the earlier one in which Ted resisted bringing in a photograph of himself.

Monday, December 6

Dear Ted,

Today I did it again. I started talking to you about an upcoming activity that Ms. Yardley had mentioned in the newsletter and at our conference. You really got irritated. It was about Important Person, an activity in which you bring to school in a special suitcase five objects that tell something about you or your family.

You announced in no uncertain terms that you had no intention of participating. I was reminded of your reluctance to bring in the photograph of yourself at the beginning of the school year.

"Why should I bring in special things in a suitcase? If they're special to me, why should I do that? It's dumb. It's stupid. I hate school. Why do I always have to do what Ms. Yardley asks?"

That was not a happy breakfast, and I was hard put to figure out how to resolve what I had started. I tried not to make things worse by countering what you said. Rather I tried simply to listen, not to change your mind about participating. You probably will do so of your own accord when you see and understand how other children handle it.

How many other parents have met with similar reactions? I remember one parent at Back-to-School Night who voiced reservations about Important Person making some children feel uncomfortable. Is that how you feel?

It's so easy to blow things out of proportion. If only Ms. Yardley knew: what began as a low-key idea to get families more involved in school has become a real hassle for this mother-son team. But whose fault is it? Certainly not the teacher's.

Sometimes I wonder if I'm too involved in what's happening at school. Maybe you want a separate life at school. I think at times I play the teacher role when I should just be the parent.

Sorry about this morning, Ted. I'll leave this Important Person business to you and Ms. Yardley.

Love,

Mom

I thought back to some of the projects and activities I had designed in my own classrooms and wondered about their impact . . . Did I create situations for children and their parents that were unnecessarily stressful or unproductive?

A few weeks later we hit another bump when Swimmy the turtle puppet came to our house for an overnight.

Friday, December 17

Dear Ms. Yardley,

What did you think of Ted's entry about Swimmy's visit to our house? I must say it was a real chore getting the words out of Ted. It wasn't that he was unhappy about having Swimmy visit. He did all the things I assume are appropriate for a 5-year-old to do with Swimmy—talked to him, introduced him to his other stuffed animals, took him in the car with us, sat him at the dinner table, took him to bed. But then to have him help me or Swimmy write about the experience? No way!

I found myself trying to cajole Ted into doing something that seemed very difficult for him to relate to. Glancing back at other children's page-long entries, I wondered how the parents had managed to help their child and why it was so difficult for me. Somehow I doubt Ted was alone in his reaction.

Ted's Mom

Perhaps parents who are teachers themselves are more prone to this kind of conflict because they tend to slip into the teacher role. In the case of Important Person, I assumed I knew what Ms. Yardley had in mind, and I wanted some assurance that Ted would participate appropriately. In the case of Swimmy, I wasn't quite sure of the point of the activity, but I felt pressured to maintain the level of response characterized by other children's entries.

I thought back to some of the projects and activities I had designed in my own classrooms and wondered about their impact on the children and their parents. It really is possible for teachers to inadvertently create situations for children and their parents that are unnecessarily stressful, unproductive, and counter to what the teacher has in mind.

Except for writing those thorny entries, I took a break from my journal during the month of December. Ms. Yardley's notes to parents, however, continued.

School Day #57
Wednesday, December 1

Today is the first day of a new month, and that means a very busy Meeting. We cleaned off our calendar and began December, filling in our birthday celebrations. We also recorded the number of days we have had of each temperature range.

It was interesting to compare the month of October with the month of November. We could tell that November was a much colder month than October. There was *great* excitement when we checked today's temperature and recorded our first "blue" day; how appropriate on the first day of December.

School Day #61
Tuesday, December 7

Worktime continues to be a favorite time in our room. During this time children have a choice of activities that include the Pretend Center, Block Corner, Art Center, and Shelf Games. Shelf Games are a collection of manipulatives, board games, and other activities. There are some assigned activities during Worktime, but there is also time for individual choices. On days when we don't have Worktime, the children really miss it. We are looking for ways to increase this precious time.

Each child in Ms. Yardley's class was paired with a Book Buddy from Mrs. Ford's third grade. The classes met once a week to read books together as well as do other activities.

School Day #64
Friday, December 10

What a delightful morning. Today Freddy's and Max's moms came in to help children with their weaving projects during Welcome time. It was great to have their help. We are really moving along!

We also had two third-graders visit us from our Book Buddy class and play Chip Trading with four kindergartners.

We have extended our Welcome time to give more time for individual projects and have shortened our Meeting. Now we do our shared reading after snack rather than as a part of Meeting time. This allows for longer discussions at Meeting without shortchanging our reading. Everyone seems to be benefiting from our reorganized morning!

It was extraordinarily interesting to see how during the busy month of December the routines established early in the school year continued or were modified to meet changing priorities and goals. Celebrating holidays, sharing family traditions, making gifts—all were integrated at appropriate times and in appropriate ways into the rhythm of the classroom. As I struggled to balance holiday preparations with my responsibilities at work and grappled with my anxieties about not spending enough time volunteering in Ted's classroom, Ms. Yardley's special note at the end of a December newsletter made me realize how attuned she was to her parents as well as to her children:

> **Special Note:** There has been lots of mention about the wonderful help we have had from parent volunteers. We are very grateful for your time and support. At the same time I want to acknowledge the parents who are not able to come into the classroom and to recognize that you too provide a tremendous amount of support to our program through the many things you do at home to help your child succeed at school. Many thanks to every parent for the many "invisible" things you do!

I appreciated her words even though I was planning to take a few personal days this year to help out in the classroom. Ted had asked if I could come, so I wanted to do it if I possibly could.

Winter

3

That winter in New England was one to remember. School closings, delayed openings, early dismissals, and a mid-January three-day holiday weekend challenged teachers to maintain the momentum of their classroom routines and important work. Ted's teacher used it as an occasion for a little problem solving.

School Day #74
Wednesday, January 5

Yesterday's snow day made today a little confusing. We had a very interesting discussion about what number to put for today as we tracked the number of days we have been in school. Do we count snow days? The "right" answer didn't seem as important as the many ideas expressed and the different ways children reasoned.

We all made book covers for the Important Books our classmates will make for us when we have our Important Person weeks.

In an earlier message, Ms. Yardley told us that the model for the Important Books is the Margaret Wise Brown story *The Important Book*. Each child would dictate something memorable about the person of the week and then illustrate the words. All the pages would then be collected into a book that the Important Person keeps as a remembrance of his or her special week.

School Day #83
Wednesday, January 19

It took us a little while to reorient ourselves after the extra-long weekend. There were many discussions about how to handle jobs and turns in the Block Corner and Pretend Center, all of which usually last a week. After all had a chance to give their ideas, we decided to extend turns and jobs into next week.

We enjoyed beginning our celebration of Barbara, who is our Important Person this week. She shared with us what she had put in the Important Suitcase. It was fun to get to know Barbara a little better.

Many children also brought in some interesting textures from home to contribute to our texture collage. At the library, Ms. Polhamus gave us some books about our sense of touch.

Special Note on Celebrating the Important Person: This week begins our Important Person project. As you may remember, each week we will celebrate a different child. Since our children have shown a tremendous interest in books, I thought it would be nice if each week the Important Person would bring in a favorite book to share with the class. A family member could come in to read the story, or I could read it, or your child could retell or read the book. Here's the plan . . .

On Monday, the week before your child's week, he or she will bring home the Important Suitcase. Your child will need to

1. Gather five special items to share at school
2. Complete, with help from an adult, a short survey found in the suitcase
3. Choose a favorite book to share at school
4. Bring to school the suitcase with special items, survey, and book on the Monday of his or her special week.

Sharing the Important Suitcase will be the kickoff to your child's week.

I remember cringing at the mention of the Important Person project and avoiding any discussion of it with Ted. Occasionally he mentioned the special items someone had revealed from the Important Suitcase or what he had said about the person for the Important Book. I casually listened, waiting to pick up clues about whether he had changed his opinion about participating. I was glad I had signed up to have Ted's week in April—a lot could happen between now and then.

Was I overly concerned about Ted's reaction to this one activity? Yes, probably. Because I was so eager for Ted to begin his school career with the right attitude about the value of participation, I ascribed a great deal of significance to his lack of interest in this particular activity.

Ms. Yardley's messages helped me focus on the big picture. While individual activities came and went, it was the significant routines and the fundamental processes of learning that were important to her. She allowed herself sufficient time to explore children's questions. She was willing to modify or alter plans if it made sense to do so. She was terrific about accepting children where they were in their learning, and she understood that her agenda might not always match theirs and that that was okay. And what a good listener and observer she seemed to be; she was truly a teacher who focused intently upon what children could do rather than focusing on what they hadn't yet mastered. She was a good role model for me as a parent trying to get better at taking my cues from Ted.

Dear Ted,

You've been doing a lot of counting lately. You seem very interested in numbers and adding them in your head. It's such fun to watch your eyes as you calculate the answer. Tonight we looked at a tour map of Boston, and you picked out all the highway route signs. You must be talking about numbers in school.

We've also been writing every now and then. You tell me the words to a story, and I write them. I can't seem to get you to do any of the phonetic spelling you do in school with Ms. Yardley.

Love,

Mom

Tuesday, January 25

Dear Ms. Yardley,

What has the class been doing in math recently? Ted counts everything! He really seems to be getting the idea of one-to-one correspondence.

Tonight before bedtime he went through every page of What Will the Weather Be Like Today? *and counted people on one page, buses on the next, umbrellas, and so forth.*

"Oh, look at this page. Listen to this!" he exclaimed. "I love this!"

At dinner time (or anytime, it seems) Ted quizzes us on addition facts with numbers of two or three digits: 20 + 20, 40 + 40, 100 + 100, 100 + 200. There is a giggle when we give the correct answer and he realizes he got it right. He's intent on visualizing everything in his head. Even when we hold up our fingers, he counts by staring intently at them; he never touches them.

Ted's excited about our new thermometer. Graphing the temperatures in class has been a meaningful activity for him. He keeps us posted about patterns the class has noticed, and he's always eager to read our thermometer.

It's so exciting to see Ted's interests, skills, and knowledge develop.

Ted's Mom

Based on what I saw during this period of time, Ted was showing an especially strong interest and development in math. I realized suddenly how important it is to appreciate each child's growth and learning on an individual basis. While a teacher follows a curriculum and focuses on certain topics and ideas at given times during the year, children receive and process information in very different ways and according to very different timetables. Probably Ms. Yardley was not doing any more in math than she usually did. Rather, it seemed, Ted was making new meanings for himself in this area based on concepts and information that clicked for him at that moment.

I realized how important it is for a teacher to revisit topics and skills again and again in a number of ways during the course of the year. Often schools get so caught up in the flurry of isolated activities that the bigger picture of what's truly important and meaningful is overlooked. I could see how easy it is for us parents, as well, to become so concerned about an individual homework assignment or spelling test or worksheet that we lose perspective on the child's overall development and learning process. I didn't want that to happen to me. I was glad to have a teacher help me see this by her example.

School Day #86
Monday, January 24

At Writing Time today children drew pictures and wrote about something that happened to them on the weekend. In our writing process we are working toward children being able to independently write the first and last letters of most words. Now at midyear many of the children can listen to a word an adult says slowly, isolate the sounds, and then identify the letters that go with the sounds. As the year goes along, the children will be able to isolate sounds independently as well as identify sounds.

School Day #87
Tuesday, January 25

Recently, when we were tracking the days, one child said, "We know how many days we have been in school. Let's find out how many hours we have been here!" What a great question, and the perfect problem for our calculators. Part of our math curriculum is learning some basics about using a calculator. As well as *how,* we want children to have an idea of *why* and *when* to use a calculator.

We describe calculator problems as "big-number problems." It is less important that the child know how to solve the problem than that the problem involve big numbers and thus be suited to the calculator. The children had fun punching in 84 (number of school days) x 3.75 (number of hours in a school day). Can you guess how many hours we have been in school? It is certainly a big number!

Was Ted that child? He's always coming up with questions like that at home. By not mentioning the child's name, Ms. Yardley let parents believe the question may have come from their child. She valued the ability to ask a good question. Ms. Yardley's curriculum was flexible in order to encourage the children to pursue issues that piqued their interest and curiosity. As she knew, questions afford learners of all ages the opportunity to assume some ownership and responsibility for their learning.

School Day #88
Wednesday, January 26

Today as we were putting up school day #86, one child noted that there are only four days until #90. That's a big day for us because it is the halfway mark of kindergarten!

We can easily see the halfway point on our number grid where we track the days we have been in school. We also talk about halfway in our schedules; we have hanging schedules, and we move an arrow down the schedule as we move from activity to activity. We can see clearly when we are halfway through our Meeting and halfway through our morning.

We also had fun this morning learning the alphabet song "A . . . Alligators All Around." We read the companion book, listened to a cassette, and watched the movie. Then many children sang the song as they pointed to the alphabet alligators hanging on the wall in our room.

> Just as children have different timetables, so do parents. There are things I am ready to hear now that wouldn't have had meaning for me earlier in the year.

Reading that last message and realizing that we were nearing the halfway point of the school year, I felt sad. Although none of my journal entries reflected the importance of the occasion, I remember how important it was to Ted. Ms. Yardley used the halfway point as an opportunity to refresh our memories about some important agendas she would continue to have for the remainder of the year. Just as children have different timetables, so do parents. There are probably things I am ready to hear now that wouldn't have had meaning for me earlier in the year. In addition to twenty different children, Ms. Yardley was also dealing with twenty sets of parents with different perspectives, expectations, anxieties, and standards.

School Day #93
Wednesday, February 2

Each week you will find a poem or song attached to the front of our newsletter. The song or poem will be one that we read that week. Please be sure to help your child share it with you. Sing or read the piece together, or let your child sing or read it alone. As your child reads, help him or her point to the words he or she is saying. This is helpful for children at all levels of literacy development.

For some children pointing to the words helps to establish left-to-right progressions and match spoken and written words. Others who are making letter/sound associations will become more focused on those associations as they say and point. And those who are beginning to develop a sight-word vocabulary will increase their knowledge as they look and point.

Most important, your child will enjoy sharing what she or he knows with you.

Ms. Yardley would have been proud of us if she had known how much fun we had with the weekly poems and songs. Each week we collected them in a special book that we read or sang from, cover to cover, whenever the spirit moved us. Ted frequently shared the collection with friends and family, proudly performing the wonderful anthology, which brought back memories of various projects and thematic studies. All were innovations of text based on familiar tunes. I appreciated how Ted's literacy development had progressed from September to January, just as Ms. Yardley had predicted.

Every now and then that year, my journal entries and Ms. Yardley's messages concerned the same topic. I found it amusing to compare notes, and I wondered what Ted's reflections would have been if he had been keeping a journal. It was not surprising that both Ms. Yardley and I remarked on the presence of a toilet in the middle of the kindergarten

classroom. It certainly would have been difficult
to fully understand the point of this activity without Ms. Yardley's communication to inform me.

Tuesday, February 8

Dear Ted,

*Do you really have a toilet in the middle of
your classroom? I want to believe you, but
somehow I can't picture it. It must be right up
your alley since you're always talking about
pipes and drains and where the water goes.*
Now you're going to find out firsthand how plumbing works.
*Tonight Dad pulled out the fix-it manual I gave him for Christmas
and read you the part about toilets. You loved it.*

Love,

Mom

School Day #97
Tuesday, February 8

Today was a very interesting day! Believe it or not, we have a
real toilet in our classroom, and we are experimenting with it to see
how it works. We are working in small groups, a different group each
day until vacation. While learning a lot about how toilets work, we
are also learning how to find out about things. We are listening carefully to each other's questions and talking about different ways to

72

find the answers. Our questions and approaches are as important as the answers we find.

Using food coloring, we were able to track where the water went when it left the tank. With paper towels we clogged the toilet and figured out how to move the clog with a plunger. We unscrewed and unhooked pieces to see what effect that had. We were amazed by the amount of water used with each flush. Much of the inquiry was stimulated by the children, and all of the discoveries were their own.

Tuesday, February 15

Dear Ms. Yardley,

Ted announced tonight, "I can't read." I'm not sure what prompted this statement. It seemed to come out of the blue as he was diving into his Valentine candy. Could it have been the little candy hearts with messages that he indeed couldn't read (except perhaps for "I Love You")?

I know that Ted can't read yet, so I'm not about to argue with him; yet something must be up. I believe children must grasp this notion in order to realize that reading is something that takes some effort to learn.

A while ago Ted was proclaiming that he could read 101 Dalmatians *when clearly he was engaged in an excellent retelling. When he recently brought home* Hearts Everywhere, *he certainly read it but wasn't about to claim that he was a reader. In fact he's been making the following, truthful distinction: "I can read some books."*

Ted's Mom

In Ms. Yardley's last communication before February vacation, the Wednesday entry had a rather long note at the end. She explained more about "A . . . Alligators All Around".

Special Note: Our class has been learning the song "A . . . Alligators All Around" from the musical *Really Rosie.* By popular vote we decided to perform this song at our school assembly on March 25 sometime between 10:30 and 11:00 o'clock. You are most welcome to come.

Please look at the bottom of this page to see what part your child has chosen. Some children wanted just to sing, and they are our Chorus. Others wanted to act out a letter. Those children will perform with a partner. For those acting out a letter, the letter is noted as well as the action.

Talk with your child about whether she or he thinks simple props are needed to act out the letter. For some, actions alone may suffice.

Send your child back to school after vacation with any ideas and props she or he has come up with. We'll talk about the ideas and see what looks good for the performance as a whole.

As with all the projects in our class, the emphasis is on the children's ideas and the process we go through to put the performance together. We'll be working out the details as we go along. We'll keep you posted.

Ted was extremely excited about this project. He had volunteered to act out three letters with a partner, and he had also volunteered our family to make a tape of the song for Ms. Yardley, who said her recording was showing signs of wear. We would certainly do that, among other things, during the upcoming February vacation. I wondered what made this particular activity one that Ted so readily embraced.

Saturday, February 26

Dear Ted,

What a great February vacation we've had together! One day we hiked around Walden Pond, and another we went to a play. You built some great block structures indoors and had fun playing outdoors in the snow. We watched a little of the Olympics each day.

We remembered to make a tape of "A . . . Alligators All Around" for Ms. Yardley, and we're both learning the words! You seem really enthusiastic about your class performance on March 25. I'll be there; Daddy hopes he can come too.

Will you tell Ms. Yardley about any of the things we've done this week? What did you like best?

Love,

Mom

Of course Ted would have occasion to tell Ms. Yardley about vacation either during Headline News or during Writing Time. I'd thought that Ted would tell her about our hike around Walden Pond or the play we saw or the fun he had playing in the snow. But when next I saw Ted's Big Black Journal, in the dated entry for vacation he had written in his own phonetic spelling simply, "I watched the Olympics."

Just as I would never know everything good and meaningful that was happening at school if Ted were my only source of information, so too Ms. Yardley would never know how rich and wonderful our vacation had been.

School Day #103
Monday, February 28

It was wonderful to see everyone again! After we had a chance to say "hello" to one another, we took out our Big Black Journals and drew pictures about something that happened over vacation. Then we wrote about it.

We continue to learn how to isolate sounds in words and then figure out what letters go with those sounds. It's a challenging and complex process, and it's been very exciting to see the children grow in their abilities.

My hunch about Ted's "I can't read" announcement had been right; it seemed he really was preparing to tackle this difficult task. I remember congratulating myself, at this point in the year, on how I too had grown in my abilities to predict and observe and listen and understand.

Spring

4

Although I went into Ted's classroom just before winter vacation to share a holiday tradition with his classmates, I was not able to do any volunteer work on a regular basis as some parents did. Ted seemed to accept this, which was good since my work made volunteering difficult. Still, I did have a few personal days I could use during the course of the year, and during the next two months I arranged to spend time in his class on three different occasions.

These opportunities provided me with firsthand knowledge of what kindergarten was like. Though I was well aware that my presence in the classroom no doubt changed the way in which Ted functioned on that particular morning, I still felt lucky to experience Ms. Yardley's classroom and share that experience with my son.

Wednesday, March 2

Dear Ted,

How great it was to visit your class on Tuesday! I loved having you show me all the things you like to do in class. We had a good time at the bean table. It was fun filling the red bucket with beans and plunging our hands to the bottom. Eventually I headed to the Publishing Center to help David with his book. At Ms. Yardley's suggestion, you walked us down to the computer lab. Then you left us to our work and returned to the classroom.

I am so proud of you. Did you find it hard to leave us? Had Ms. Yardley prepared you for this?

Next time, when I come in April, I get to work with you!

Love,

Mom

Having parents volunteer in meaningful ways is highly valued in most schools for a variety of reasons. Volunteers allow children to receive much more individual help and attention. Having other adults in a classroom in addition to the teacher validates the importance of children's work. Ms. Yardley, I think, saw volunteering as a concrete way to forge a partnership with parents. It was another way to help us understand the reality of her kindergarten classroom and its inhabitants and be enriched by working with our children.

I wondered what value I placed on volunteering in my son's classroom. I believed I was doing it partly for Ted, partly for myself, and partly for Ms. Yardley. Ted often told me that some of his friends' parents had spent the morning in his classroom and that it would be fun to have me do the same. There was so much to do, and, as he said, it would be easier for him to show me than to tell me. I think Ted simply enjoyed sharing his school world with me and took pleasure in my reaction. As for me, I wanted to show both Ted and Ms. Yardley how much I valued their classroom and how much I appreciated the opportunity to pitch in and help. Their classroom was an important place, and volunteering my time was one small way to show how I felt.

Although it was not clear to me in September, Ted's first year at public school marked the beginning of *my* learning how to separate from my child

> Ted's first year at school marked the beginning of *my* learning how to separate from my child in more ways than just leaving him each day.

in more ways than just leaving him at his classroom each day. In my initial musings about how my son was adjusting to school, I had marveled at how much information he picked up not only about the workings of his classroom but about how the school was run as well. These reflections continued throughout the year.

Wednesday, March 9

Dear Ted,

Today Donna finally got her new school bus. You've anticipated this for quite some time and have told us in great detail what the new bus would be like.

I am intrigued by how deeply invested you are in so much of the life at Bowman School. You're really concerned with all that happens, and you make it your business to find out the details of the school's operation. I remember how comfortable you used to feel at your child care program, and now in a few short months you seem to feel the same way at Bowman. It's Dad and I who don't yet feel at home. Public school seems to be more of an adjustment for us.

Love,

Mom

It's Dad and I who don't yet feel at home. Public school seems to be more of an adjustment for us.

How many adjustments life continually challenges us to make! Why are adjustments easier for some people to make than for others?

On a family drive one Sunday afternoon, Ted announced that he wouldn't be going to first grade. Bob turned to me wondering what had brought this on, and I could tell he was trying to figure out how best to respond. I too was taken aback, but as I thought about it, I realized Ted was probably just anticipating the future adjustment to first grade and signaling his concern.

The incident triggered in me the thought that I too would be adjusting again soon. As a first-time parent I had no prior knowledge to inform or reassure me—only my journal and pen to help me work things out.

Dear Ted,

Yesterday you announced that you might not go on to first grade. You explained that some children don't and that that's okay, and you thought you'd like another year in kindergarten. I wonder if a particular incident precipitated this.

Your comment started me thinking about what kind of classroom would be good for you next year. I want your first-grade teacher to have a good knowledge of child development—knowledge that he or she can use to facilitate learning in ways that are thoughtful, purposeful, and developmentally appropriate. I want your teacher to respect individual learning styles and create a classroom environment in which all children can succeed. I'd hate to have you endure the worksheets typical of all too many classrooms and the often mindless activities that are ends in themselves. Of course I want you to get a good start in reading and writing and to continue the work you've begun in math.

I'm sure Ms. Yardley has insights about the teacher and classroom environment that would suit you best. I feel reassured when I realize that Ms. Yardley will have an important role in your first-grade placement and that I will be able to share my concerns with her. We have complementary pieces of knowledge about you as a learner.

Love,

Mom

In March a major focus in Ms. Yardley's classroom was the upcoming performance of "A . . . Alligators All Around." Again Ms. Yardley took advantage of the opportunity to reinforce her goals for the project.

School Day #117
Tuesday, March 15

We are busy practicing our "A . . . Alligators All Around" song. It is very funny! You can hear us singing the song in the hall when getting on our outdoor clothes and, most important, while we're writing! We have letters and sound associations right on the tips of our tongues!

We play with language and sounds in other ways too. Today we picked the sound of *h* and substituted that sound for the first letter in our names. Understanding that words are made of separate sounds is an important concept for reading and writing, so we practice isolating sounds in the playful context of songs, poems, and games.

> Understanding that words are made of separate sounds is an important concept for reading and writing, so we practice isolating sounds in the playful context of songs, poems, and games.
> —Ms. Yardley

School Day #119
Friday, March 18

Today we practiced "A . . . Alligators All Around" on the stage in the gym. It's looking great. We continue to make changes as children add their ideas and confirm which roles they want. Truly a work in progress!

We are also having fun in our pizza shop. Did you know you can now order a pepperoni-and-mushroom pizza from the talented chefs in our classroom? Our Pretend Center has become a pizza shop. Felt slices of crust, sauce, cheese, and toppings make it possible to really have it your way! When you are in the room ask for a slice.

Friday, March 18

Dear Ted,

It's exciting to see how much you're noticing letters and words now. When we're riding in the car, you continue to spell words you see and ask what they say. Tonight you noticed Shell, Mobil, McDonald's, Speed Limit, *and* One Way. *There was one word you knew already:* Pizza. *I think I know why.*

I'm curious to know what you're doing in school during Writing Time. I look forward to seeing your Writing Folder at my next conference with Ms. Yardley.

Love,

Mom

Ms. Yardley's
weekly notes
to parents
played an
important part
in helping me
understand
the context
of activities
and recognize
different
agendas.

School Day #124
Friday, March 25

What a great day! I was so proud of the wonderful performance the children gave today at assembly. They worked hard for weeks sharing ideas, solving problems, and rehearsing their parts. Most of what the audience saw today came from the children; their creativity and perseverance were remarkable. Thanks to all who were able to make it. For those who couldn't come, we are hoping to have a video to share with you.

As a teacher I'm not sure I ever understood what a thrill it is for parents to attend a performance of any kind at school. My first responsibility is to the children, so I have always structured events that will have meaning for them. I sometimes wondered whether it was worthwhile for parents to take time off from work for an event that might take longer to get to than to watch. Ms. Yardley left that decision to us in the supportive, inviting style that has become her trademark.

I would not have missed Ted's kindergarten performance for anything in the world. I could think of no better way to show not only Ted but his teacher as well how much I valued and appreciated the work they do in school. There was no doubt in my mind, though, that Ms. Yardley's weekly

> I found Ted's portfolio of written work a delight. How much more meaningful it is to review within its context the work a child has done over time rather than to see isolated pieces brought home sporadically.

notes to parents played an important part in helping me understand the context and recognize different agendas that were operative here.

Parent conference time, scheduled for the end of March, was yet another opportunity for me to understand Ted's kindergarten experience.

Tuesday, March 29

Dear Ms. Yardley,

I can't believe we have our spring conference this week and that among other issues we will broach the subject of first-grade placement.

Which first-grade classroom will be best for Ted? Drawing on your knowledge of him as a learner and a person, what kind of environment would suit him? Which teacher would be a good match for him? I also have to ask who would be a good match for me, *even though that issue probably should not be paramount. I can't deny that you are exactly the kind of teacher I imagined Ted having for his kindergarten year.*

I hope you can help me figure out my role in the placement process. You of course know more about Ted's needs as a learner. You know more about his school personality and style of interaction. You know more about the first-grade teachers. You know more about the school's concerns for creating balanced classes that will meet the needs of all children.

Because of my work in schools, my role as a parent is complicated by my firsthand knowledge of how difficult the placement process is. In the abstract, I would prefer a teacher whose philosophy of education is congruent with mine. However, I'm not confident that educational philosophy is the overriding factor in the choice of a teacher who is best suited to Ted, so I will rely on your judgment. I trust you to decide in which classroom Ted would thrive.

Ted's Mom

As it turned out, the subject of placement didn't come up for the simple reason that the purpose of the conference was to discuss Ted's progress and there was lots to talk about and a great deal to see.

Dear Ms. Yardley,

Once again I enjoyed talking with you. You described the Ted I know but also offered insights about how he's doing academically—a perspective that I avoid at home even though I am sometimes tempted to look at Ted through my teacher eyes. You spoke knowledgeably, honestly, and fondly about him. Clearly you know the feelings parents have for their children and how vulnerable we are to what teachers say about them.

I found Ted's portfolio of written work a delight. How much more meaningful it is to review within its context the work a child has done over time rather than to see isolated pieces brought home sporadically, then misplaced, forgotten, or discarded. There's been quite a change since September, and I'm excited about having Ted's work for my own at the end of the year. I hope Ted's teachers each year will maintain such a portfolio. The Big Black Journal that will follow him through his years at Bowman School is a treasure too.

Then there's the issue of the three-page conference form with those 1s, 2s, and 3s indicating levels of skill competence: consistent, general, and emerging. Although I am familiar with the form—it is similar to one my school is piloting this year—it was a very different experience to be on the receiving end. While I certainly understand the intent of the approach, and while the numbers conform to the Ted we both *know, I am quite overwhelmed by the assortment of skills reported, the numbers associated with each, and what they indicate. Should I be concerned that some areas were reported as only emerging? Do I have cause for worry because my son doesn't have all 1s and 2s?*

Fortunately your comments and Ted's work samples give me a far clearer picture of Ted's growth than do the numbers. Your words were positive yet sincere. As a teacher I have a new appreciation for the anxiety parents experience at report-card and conference time.

Time ran out before we could talk about first-grade placement. I'm not sure what I would have said except to ask you which teacher you think might be a good match for Ted, although I know that would have put you on the spot. I may put my ideas in a letter to you and the principal, both to clarify my thinking and to explain my priorities. Then I'll feel that I've done what I can to ensure that the right spot will be found for Ted. You see, I believe the teacher really does make a difference.

On the other hand, I believe that in a good school there are many different kinds of "good" teachers. Is Bowman a good school? Can I be confident that any teacher given a well-balanced class will be good for Ted?

You've been a wonderful teacher for Ted and a source of tremendous support to me. I know that as next year unfolds, I'll have to strive to understand his new teacher's way of doing things.

Ted's Mom

> I'm beginning to see how important it is to Ted to have a school life about which I do not know every detail.

April was another happy, busy, productive month in Ms. Yardley's kindergarten. Field trips were scheduled and special school events were held to bring the school community closer together. At the end of the month, Ted was celebrated as the Important Person of the week.

It struck me that when April vacation arrived, the school year would wind down rapidly and my anxiety about next year would set in; but in the meantime all was right with the world. Spring was coming. Ted was talkative about school and again seemed to be in a period of equilibrium.

School Day #130
Monday, April 4

Today was the first school day of April, so we had a lot of record keeping to do. We saw a dramatic change in our temperature records. In February there were six days of "purple" temperatures (below 12 degrees), and in March there was none! Spring arrived!

We also read a new poem called "Rain Everywhere" and a new Big Book called *I Like the Rain!*

School Day #131
Tuesday, April 5

Today we went to the Science Discovery Museum with the other four kindergarten classes. We had the museum to ourselves! It was interesting and a lot of fun to explore the many hands-on activities, including a woodworking area and an art center. We also experimented with pendulums, gravity, sound, motion, and heat.

I was very proud of our children. They were full of enthusiasm yet well behaved and respectful of the materials. I was also very grateful and thankful to have the parent volunteers who chaperoned. Many, many thanks.

Tuesday, April 5

Dear Ms. Yardley,

Ted came home bubbling over with things to tell me about the Discovery Museum. We've only been to the Children's Museum, so it's clear to me that this was a real treat for him. He loves to tell me things I don't know about.

Ted's like that about his school too. Sometimes I think he believes I know too much about schools in general because I'm a teacher. He's visited my school and has a sense of how I spend my day. Yet when he compares Bowman to Alcott, as he often does, Ted makes it clear to me how different they are. I'm beginning to see how important it is to him to have a school life about which I do not know every detail.

Ted's Mom

Following the successful work on letters and sounds through the "A . . . Alligators All Around" project, Ms. Yardley helped the children make ABC Books. She seemed to have a knack for introducing a project or a task at just the right time—at least this one was right for Ted.

School Day #132
Wednesday, April 6

Today was another interesting day. Ms. Grant, our intern from Boston University, led a pizza-making activity. She worked with one small group of children (the others will have their turns over the next few weeks). First the children studied the recipe, and then, equipped with order forms, the children each asked a few other children what they wanted on their pizzas. They took the orders back to the pizza-making table, assembled each order, baked the pizzas, and served them to the class. They sure were delicious. You will know when your child has worked on this project because a recipe will be attached to the newsletter.

Jack's mom also joined us and worked with some children on ABC Books while others began work on individual books called "Rain Everywhere." Your child's copy should be attached to this newsletter. Please ask your child to read it to you. Thanks!

Thursday, April 7

Dear Ms. Yardley,

How proud Ted was of his ABC Book. He read it to us after we finished dinner. He told us how he had made it and colored the pictures and what a big project it was. It made a deep impression on him. What a great idea!

Ted loved making pizza, and we're going to try the recipe you sent home. The poems have been great too. Because Friday evenings tend to be our pizza nights, Ted will have plenty of occasions to practice the pizza poems. I have one memorized to take the edge off the next inevitable pizza accident:

> *I am a pizza, peppers on top,*
> *Out of the oven, into the box.*
> *Into the car and upside down,*
> *I am a pizza dropped on the ground.*
> *I was a pizza, I was the best.*
> *I was a pizza, now I'm a mess!*

Ted's Mom

Ms. Yardley provided many such opportunities to help parents connect literacy experiences at school with events at home. When I took a genuine interest in a song or poem Ted had learned or a recipe he had made, he realized how important his work with Ms. Yardley was.

School Day #134
Friday, April 8

Today at our primary assembly, we met our community's tree warden. He is helping Bowman with a very exciting project. As a school we will plant 17 trees along Philip Road and Bowman's driveway in celebration of Arbor Day on April 29. After planting we will be responsible for watering the new trees.

Friday, April 8

Dear Ms. Yardley,

Sometimes Ted sounds like he owns Bowman School. Today he came home talking about the trees that the children would be planting around the school grounds and how the kindergarten classes will have a special area they'll be responsible for.

Ted really cares about the school and has come to see his place there as more than merely that of a student in your classroom. My interest has focused on your classroom, but Ted has been working to make sense of the entire school community. He talks frequently about the weekly assembly programs; about David, his third-grade Book Buddy; and about the rest of Mrs. Ford's third-grade class. He pays attention to the principal's whereabouts and has formed opinions about her role in the school.

Ted reports excitedly about new equipment or materials that appear in the gym or in your classroom. He observes relationships between the special-area teachers and the classroom teachers he knows. He never fails to mention something about the custodians or a task in which they were engaged and why it was important.

Ted knows his way around the school and takes pride in suggesting alternate routes when we are there together. He knows the routines and rules and procedures. In short, he feels at home. I'm amazed at how quickly this happens.

Ted's Mom

Thus April vacation began on a positive note.

The week school reopened would be a busy one: school pictures on Monday, an opportunity for Bob and me to spend time in Ted's classroom on Tuesday during his Important Person week, a field trip to Mario's Restaurant to make pizza on Thursday, and Arbor Day on Friday.

Sunday, April 24

Dear Ted,

What a wonderful vacation we had together this week. I was on your wavelength, and it felt great. On Sunday morning we got five items together for your Important Suitcase. In January you said you wouldn't participate, but today you seemed pretty enthusiastic—especially when Dad said you could take his trumpet to school!

You picked some great objects to share; they told a lot about you: a collage of photos you selected yourself, your catcher's mitt, the Pinocchio finger puppets you enjoy playing with, Dad's trumpet (which you love to get ahold of whenever you go up to the attic), and a book of bedtime stories that you keep on the night table beside your bed. I hope you won't be too shy.

Love,

Mom

School Day #140
Monday, April 25

It was wonderful to see everyone back at school. Everyone chatted briefly and then got right to work on new entries in their Big Black Journals. There were many ideas exchanged and discussed. April vacation often seems to be the beginning of a very exciting time—dance recitals, T-ball practice, vacation memories.

Then we had our pictures taken, which turned our day upside down, and we *ended* the day with Meeting. But everyone looked beautiful!

Monday, April 25

Dear Ms. Yardley,

 When you first described the Important Person project, I had some misgivings about how interested Ted was going to be in participating. Remember the photograph he wouldn't put on the bulletin board for several weeks at the start of school? Remember the rather brief entry we made in Swimmy's journal? I don't have to go on! I selected a week in April as Ted's week to give him ample time to get used to the idea and to see how the others handled it.

 Although we had vacation week to think about the project, we saved it for Sunday morning. Getting the suitcase packed was really a collaborative venture. Bob and I were especially careful that Ted be the one primarily invested in it. We took turns helping him. We wanted him to realize that we thought the project was important and we took it seriously but that it was his project, not ours. Parent involvement is a delicate balancing act.

 I'm curious about how Ted presented the objects. How much did he say? Did he convey accurate information? What did he embellish?

 When I come in to Ted's classroom tomorrow, I can share some time with him. I wanted to plan an activity that included some other children, but Ted wasn't comfortable with anything I suggested. I sense that certain activities he and I enjoy at home Ted doesn't feel like sharing with others—cooking, putting together jigsaw puzzles, drawing, doing art projects, playing games.

I found it hard not to push projects I wanted to do, but the question would then be, For whom am I doing them? I often see parents at my school doing things more for themselves, even though they think they're doing them for the child. I hope I'm not overreacting and going to the opposite extreme.

Ted's dad will read a story to the class. I'll offer to help children with their writing because Ted knows that's what I do in my work and thinks it's a good idea. Of course I'll also help Ted publish his story, and I hope that will go smoothly.

Ted's Mom

Fortunately the decisions we made in preparation for Ted's Important Person week seemed to be the right ones. Ted participated eagerly, and Bob and I had a great time.

Tuesday, April 26

Dear Ms. Yardley,

It was wonderful to be in your classroom today. I was glad to help Ted publish his book about the Boston Marathon as well as help other children work on their journal entries. I'm impressed that Bowman School has made a tradition of having children keep those Big Black

Journals. I'm curious about how the tradition began and how it's used by different teachers.

Isn't Ted's dad a great storyteller? He and Ted love The Giant Who Threw Tantrums, *so I wasn't surprised that they selected that story. I had no idea Bob would ham it up like he did. I could feel Ted's pride at having his dad share some of himself with the children. Do you understand Ted better and appreciate him more after observing and talking with his mom and dad? What have you learned about Ted through us?*

How did Ted fare when he shared the items he brought in the Important Suitcase? Did he talk about the photos? The process of selection was fun to watch. Did he expand on them, or was he shy? And how about the trumpet? Did he blast away on it? Clearly, sharing the trumpet was the high point of the experience for Ted.

It was so hard, especially at the beginning of the year, to get anything out of Ted at the end of the day. Even now when he talks about school, he shares what he wants to share, and it's not always the topic I want to hear about. I mean, while I appreciate listening to anything Ted has to say, I also have some questions and areas of interest of my own. It is important for parents to understand, however, that their child is a separate person and that one of the challenges of parenting is learning when and how to let go a little bit. Kindergarten has given me the opportunity to take some steps in what might be a lifelong process.

Ted's Mom

School Day #141
Tuesday, April 26

Today we were lucky to have both Ted's mom and his dad visit us. Ted's mom helped Ted publish his story and then stayed and helped many children with their writing. Ted's dad read a wonderful monster story from one of Ted's favorite books. Many thanks, Irene and Bob.

We also had fun trying to figure out what a new funny-looking machine in our classroom will be used for. After several wonderful guesses (weather station, popcorn popper, animal cage), the children got it. It's an incubator!

Next week we will put a dozen fertile chicken eggs in our incubator. Hopefully they will hatch in three weeks!

Ms. Yardley made the most of a class field trip by having the children take public transportation. While Ted left that morning excited at the prospect of having pizza as his mid-morning snack, the 25¢ fare he carried in his pocket for the bus ride was also an important part of the experience.

School Day #143
Thursday, April 28

Today at about ten o'clock we walked to the LEXPRESS bus and rode to Lexington Center and then walked to Mario's Restaurant. We went into the kitchen and watched the chefs make some pizzas. A conveyor belt took the pizzas through the oven. When the pizzas came out the other side seven minutes later, they were hot and bubbly! We had a good time enjoying the results.

> Ted's mom helped him publish his story, and Ted's dad read a wonderful monster story.
> —Ms. Yardley

While field trips and chicks were sure signs of spring, so were Arbor Day and a beautification project for Bowman School.

School Day #144
Friday, April 29

Today was Arbor Day, and we celebrated in several ways. First we read *Miss Rumphius* and talked about ways we could make the world a better place, as Miss Rumphius did in the story.

Later in the morning we participated in a schoolwide planting project. A group of parents received a grant to purchase 17 trees and some plants and shrubs. The plants and shrubs were planted around the Bowman School sign. This is the area the kindergartners are responsible for maintaining. With Mrs. White's help the entire kindergarten made a sign that reads Kinder Garden, and each child put his or her thumbprint on it. We pledged to take care of these valuable plants.

Ted took this responsibility to heart, although it was several weeks before I realized it. One afternoon when I picked up Ted from extended day, he noticed that one of the stakes providing support for a newly planted tree was broken. After talking about what possibly could have happened, Ted decided that someone should be told about it. He proceeded to track down one of the custodians, who listened intently. The custodian assured Ted that someone would replace the stake, and within a few days someone had. Ted informed me of the repair.

Endings

5

In May Ted would turn 6. May was also the month in which the eggs were expected to hatch. Ted was thrilled to think that he might share his birthday with the chicks. While end-of-the-year activities would begin by the end of the month, until then Ms. Yardley continued to highlight the important learning in which she and the children were engaged.

School Day #147
Wednesday, May 4

Today we carefully put 12 fertile eggs in our incubator—our "electric hen." The incubator will keep our eggs warm and moist and will turn them regularly, just like a mother hen. Our job is to check the temperature and count the days. Incubation takes about 21 days, so we expect our eggs to hatch close to Ted's birthday on May 25.

We are all becoming interested in the small, "predictable" books in our classroom. For many children they are the first step into reading. The patterned texts give beginning readers the support they need to learn to read them quickly. Children are able to practice strategies essential to independent reading such as matching spoken words with printed words and using pictures and beginning sounds to figure out words. Children enjoy taking them home to read with their family. If a small book comes home, read it once with your child while she or he points to the words. Then ask your child to read and point alone. Many thanks!

Giving children the right amount of support at the emergent reading level is always a challenge. Ms. Yardley seemed to find the right balance within the broader context of her kindergarten program by using the third-grade Book Buddies as a supportive audience.

School Day #148
Thursday, May 5

Today we did something new and special with our Book Buddies. Just before meeting with them, each child picked out a small book or a Big Book and practiced reading it. When our Book Buddies came, instead of having the third-graders read to the kindergartners, the kindergartners read to the third-graders!

Every kindergartner is able to read at least one book in our classroom! We have been practicing together, and some children have taken books home. It is very exciting to see the children's growth.

School Day #149
Friday, May 6

We worked hard today to add the finishing touches to our Mother's Day books. I was touched by the stories the children told me and their Book Buddies, who helped with this project. It was memorable to me to hear how the most important time the children spent with their moms was doing simple things together like playing cards or swinging on a swing set. I chuckled too to hear how many children felt that the thing their moms like to do best is sleep! I'm sure you don't get nearly the rest you really need! In any case, Moms, you are a special group, and we hope you enjoy our stories.

A Book
about
Moms

by Ms. Yardley's
Kindergartners

Bowman School

Ted's
Mom

My Mom liKes to swim. when I am with my mom I liKe to Cook. My Mom is A teacher. Sometimes I get to go to her schooL with her. When my Mom is home she liKes to Kiss my Dad.

Sunday, May 8

Dear Ted,

What a wonderful Mother's Day present you made for me. I enjoyed reading your thoughts about me as well as the thoughts your classmates expressed about their mothers. Ms. Yardley is right: it's the simple things we do together that make a difference—for me as well as for you.

Love,
Mom

It was surprising to hear one day that kindergartners would have homework. This was not Ms. Yardley's invention but rather a component of a schoolwide mathematics program. The program seemed to fit with Ms. Yardley's approach to teaching, but most important, the assignments encouraged children to take some initiative and responsibility. The homework reinforced newly learned skills and concepts and provided additional thinking and practice time at each child's pace. It also gave parents a better idea of the mathematics children were learning at school.

Monday, May 9

Dear Ted,

You announced that you had "homework" tonight as soon as I picked you up at extended day. You had the folder Home Link in your backpack and explained quite well what the task was. You took the idea of homework seriously; we did it together. "Count the books on your bottom shelf." You counted 70. Then I suggested you put the folder back in your backpack yourself.

I'm trying to get you to organize yourself a bit—to put your lunch box in your backpack each morning, to remember your library book each Tuesday evening, and so forth. Sometimes moms who are very organized have children who are disorganized because the moms do all the organization. I don't want that to happen to us.

The Home Link™ idea seems like a good one for you. Because you seem to love math, you'll probably enjoy the tasks, and I'll enjoy working with you.

Love,
Mom

School Day #152
Wednesday, May 11

Today we candled some brown chick eggs and some white ones. The darker eggs are harder to see through, so we try them later than the white eggs, when they are further developed.

Max's mom came in to read with some children. Many children drew pictures and wrote about what they had drawn. One child read the story she had written to the class. Other children played a math game called Chip Trading.

I am sending home another Home Link. We are enjoying sharing the results of our "math homework" together.

School Day #153
Thursday, May 12

Today we had another interesting day with our Book Buddies. Like last week, the kindergartners chose Big Books or small, predictable books to share with their buddies. Then the kindergartners drew pictures and dictated sentences to their buddies that described their pictures. The third-graders wrote the sentences on oaktag strips and then cut apart each word. The kindergartners then put the words in the correct order, glued them to their pictures, and read the sentences to their Book Buddies. The buddies worked wonderfully together.

Saturday, May 14

Dear Ms. Yardley,

Your newsletter was chockfull again this week. Woven through the class news were messages to increase our understanding of your educational approach and the curriculum. I was prepared to read between the lines because of a meeting I had attended in my own school system about parent-teacher communication. Newsletters were high on the list of methods everyone believed could make a difference in giving parents not only the information they want but the information teachers want parents to have about the process of educating their children. I once again realize how valuable your communication has been to me this year.

Now I find myself thinking about next year (and the next and the next). I know that kindergarten teachers are probably the best communicators and, next to child care providers, have the most contact with parents. They see it as an integral part of their job. They view children as whole people, and if any grade level in a school reflects holistic, developmentally appropriate practice, it is without a doubt kindergarten. To some extent good kindergarten teachers spoil parents. You've spoiled me!

What a different school experience parents and children might have if fourth- and fifth-grade teachers communicated with parents in a similar fashion. Or how about even first- and second-grade teachers?

What happens to parent-teacher communication as children get older? Imagine if certain practices set forth at the kindergarten level became standard operating procedure throughout the elementary grades—and maybe even into middle school. What a wonderful school world that might be!

Ted's Mom

It seemed only fitting that during the month of May Ms. Yardley finally would receive a letter from me. Of course she didn't know about the many undelivered ones I had written during the year. Writing to Ted and Ms. Yardley without their receiving the letters, or even knowing about them, sometimes felt a bit strange—or maybe just incomplete. I did want to send a letter to Ms. Yardley, and the occasion that I took to do it was Teacher Appreciation Week.

Sunday, May 15

Dear Ms. Yardley,

Though I am a teacher, I never fully valued Teacher Appreciation Week until this year—the year my son Ted began his public school career. I never before understood the depth of gratitude a parent can feel for a teacher who creates a classroom environment that enables children to love learning, to exhibit genuine enthusiasm and excitement for purposeful and meaningful tasks, and to experience a feeling of belonging to a new community of friends. All this you have done for Ted, and more.

I understand, value, trust, and, yes, deeply appreciate you as a teacher, a person, a parent, and a friend. Ted has had a gloriously happy and productive year. Thank you for making it so.

Sincerely,

Irene Hannigan

. . . the depth of gratitude for a teacher who creates a classroom environment that enables children to love learning, to exhibit genuine enthusiasm for meaningful tasks, and to experience belonging to a new community of friends.

As I composed this letter, I had a flashback to late August when I had found my eyes filling with tears at the prospect of Ted beginning kindergarten. It had seemed then as though everywhere I looked, I found yet another moving article by a mother anticipating her child's break from her. I read them all. Some were sappy, some manipulative, some poignant, and some rang true. Secretly I had cried; outwardly I had prepared myself for the beginning of school.

Now, as the end of Ted's kindergarten year approached, I realized that there would be more private tears. I would experience another transition with no particular preparation for dealing with it. Like first-time parents bringing a newborn home from the hospital, we receive few instructions relative to the magnitude of the event. We are left to figure things out for ourselves. Of course life doesn't just come to a halt while we take the time we need to learn. It's on-the-job training, and we must make the time while coping with all the competing demands life places on us.

Monday, May 23

Dear Ted,

   The next few weeks of school will be filled with end-of-the-year activities. You mentioned twice that you are working on your last self-portrait. How does that make you feel? I imagine you'll be bringing them all home soon. I'm looking forward to seeing them together and discussing with you the ways in which they've changed during the course of the year.

   You are acting different lately, engaging in baby talk and fake crying when you don't get your way and sometimes shedding real tears for no obvious reason. I'm curious about how you're behaving in school. Is it because your birthday's right around the corner? Are you excited?

   I vaguely remember this happening before you turned 5 and before your 4th birthday as well. It makes me appreciate how relatively easy things usually are with you. Hopefully this too shall pass.

Love,

Mom

As Ted anxiously anticipated his 6th birthday, his class awaited the arrival of the chicks.

School Day #161
Tuesday, May 24

Today was the 21st day of the chicks' incubation. Throughout the day we anxiously peered into the incubator, but there were no signs of pecking. We have turned off the egg turner because the chicks are so big inside their shells that it would not be comfortable for them to be turned. They are also positioning themselves to be able to peck their way out. Today they have probably broken through the air sac and gasped their first breath.

Wednesday, May 25

Dear Ted,

> *Oh, what a beautiful morning!*
> *Oh, what a beautiful day!*
> *Today is Ted's birthday,*
> *We wish him the best today!*

While getting dressed this morning I heard this tune coming from your room, probably in anticipation of your class singing it to you today at Meeting.

While hopping around on the bed, you discovered the number 6 in your underpants and were quite amazed at the coincidence. Home Link really must be making an impression. How pleased Ms. Yardley would be if she knew. There are so many things teachers never know about children's learning.

Happy birthday, Ted! Now you are 6.

Love,

Mom

School Day #162
Wednesday, May 25

How excited we were to come in today and see that four chicks had begun to peck their way out! We had a "chick watch" all day with small groups of children watching the chicks' progress.

The chicks need to peck a ring completely around the wide end of the shell near the air sac. Then with one great effort they push the end of the shell and flop out. They are usually so exhausted from their work that they lie wet and tired on the bottom of the incubator for several hours.

Today the chicks had pecked only small holes in their eggs. We could hear them peeping and see their beaks moving, but they will not actually emerge until after the children have left school for the day.

We did celebrate today as the chicks' birthday. Ted, who also had a birthday today, was kind enough to share his special day with the chicks!

School Day #163
Thursday, May 26

Today when we arrived six little chicks greeted us! Three were already dry and fluffy, so they were ready to be moved to the brooder we had made for them. (The brooder is two cardboard boxes taped together with one area open and one area sheltered. There is a light in the sheltered area to keep the chicks warm.) The other three chicks were still damp and needed to stay in the incubator until they dried. We were able to pat one gently, and we talked about the chicks' needs and how we will care for them.

Our Book Buddies came later in the morning to see the chicks; in fact many classes came to visit! We shared books with our buddies, and then they helped us to do a writing-and-drawing paper that sequenced the chicks' development.

Attached to today's newsletter you'll find an interesting edition of *Super Science* about eggs. I hope you will enjoy it at home!

Once again Ms. Yardley showed how connected and purposeful her teaching and classroom were. The Book Buddies shared in the chick-hatching project by helping their kindergarten friends reflect on the process they had recently witnessed. And the monthly science newsletter, which was not usually sent home with kindergartners, was sent this month because it was particularly relevant.

Friday, May 27

Dear Ted,

You were confident that the chicks would hatch and, lo and behold, they did! So far 6 out of 12. Not bad. You said they did most of their work during the night, but there was plenty to see during the day as well. Now they're in a cozy box near the Meeting area.

> ## Birth Announcement
>
> The proud parents in Room 28 are very pleased to announce the successful hatching of 7 ~~six~~ healthy chicks!
> Names to be decided soon!
>
> Visiting Hours
> 8:30-8:50 & 11:30-12:15

Last night you wanted to read a few of the books you've brought home during the last few months. Although you still are reluctant to point to the words, you're comfortable about letting me do that part. I liked the way you focused your attention on the print and made predictions by looking at the first letter of a word. It's so tricky sometimes for me to work with you. I don't want to jeopardize my relationship with you by overdoing the teacher role.

I wonder how much parents need to work with children at home to assure appropriate progress. I don't believe children can possibly get all the attention and practice they need at school, so some home "work" has got to be beneficial. The challenge, it seems to me, is knowing what children need and how to offer it in a supportive manner.

I like it when Ms. Yardley sends work home. You're much more willing to do it when she asks you. If teachers only realized the power they had!

Love,

Mom

121

For those whose lives are oriented to an academic calendar, Memorial Day weekend marks the beginning of the final chapter of the year. End-of-the-year parties are planned, final projects are completed, farewells are anticipated, and dreams of summer vacation begin distracting everyone.

School Day #172
Thursday, June 9

We enjoyed a performance put on by some of the first- and second-grade classes today. It was a musical called *Reading Rainbow*.

Today was the last day with our Book Buddies. We celebrated the friendships we had made and the time we'd spent together by making cards for each other, listening to a story about friendship, and then eating yummy cupcakes outside and having recess together. The Book Buddies program has been a wonderful experience for both classes; we've made new friends and enjoyed a lot of books together.

Tomorrow we will say good-bye to our chicks. They are quite good at flying out of their box when the top is not on, and they really need the open space of a farmyard. We have become very attached to them, and it will be sad to see them go. It will be nice, however, to think of them running free at their farm.

Note: We will spend the next few weeks bringing closure to this school year that we have had with this wonderful group of children. We will talk about our memories and the good times we have shared as well as our worries and hopes for the next school year. On the last day of school I have two books and a special certificate to give to each child. Please let me know if your child will be leaving school before Tuesday, June 28, so we can be sure to give him or her the books and certificate and say good-bye. Thank you!

Friday, June 10

Dear Ms. Yardley,

The final section of your June 9 entry, in which you discussed bringing closure to the school year, brought tears to my eyes. As I read the part about "memories and the good times we have shared as well as our worries and hopes for the next school year," it dawned on me how much I will miss you. How do parents reach closure at the end of the school year?

Ted hasn't talked very much about next year. You've said he's very talkative in school, so I can only imagine that he shares those thoughts with you and his peers. I'm glad he has the opportunity.

I was tickled by how excited Ted was this afternoon at school when he spotted you and your daughter getting into your car in the parking lot. He's already told me that he's planning to visit you next year.

Ted's Mom

Saturday, June 11

Dear Ted,

The school year is drawing to a close. Ms. Yardley says the next few weeks' activities will bring closure. You haven't mentioned recently that you'd like to spend another year in kindergarten, so I assume you've realized the time has come to move on. What do you think first grade will be like?

You've had exactly the kind of kindergarten experience I wanted for you. I hope you found it as satisfying as I did.

Love,

Mom

School Day #173
Friday, June 10

What would you make if you had a pile of empty toilet paper rolls, Styrofoam meat trays, and other assorted junk? That's the kind of stuff that stocks our Art Center, and here are some of the creative inventions from children in our class: a video camera complete with videotape, a playground for the chicks with an elaborate slide, a hamster cage with hamsters, and much, much more.

What would you make if you had a pile of empty toilet paper rolls and assorted junk? . . . Some of the creative inventions from children: a video camera, a playground for chicks, a hamster cage with hamsters.

—Ms. Yardley

While Ted loved blocks and Legos, he also enjoyed building with bottle caps, Popsicle sticks, corks, and toothpicks. One Saturday afternoon earlier in the year, he and Bob had made a boat out of corks and toothpicks, and Ted had decided that Ms. Yardley should see it. I remember how we helped him carefully wrap it so it would make the trip to school in one piece. Ted knew Ms. Yardley would appreciate it—and she did.

School Day #174
Monday, June 13

Today was a lot of fun! We scrubbed the pool we had used for playing with the chicks, dragged it out onto the back step, and filled it with water. Then we threw all kinds of materials into the water—funnels, plastic tubing, turkey basters, paint brushes, balloons—and played and experimented the whole morning long! Many interesting questions were raised, and there was a lot of group and individual problem solving.

Not everyone got a turn to play at the pool today, but that's okay because it's going to be a hot week, so we'll set up the pool every day. Many who were not in the pool were busy making boats and other floating vehicles out of corks, toothpicks, and Styrofoam meat trays. When their turns come, these children will be ready to try out their creations.

We also read the Big Books *Hattie and the Fox* and *Up the Tree* and then made a list of our favorite Big Books this year. We have read a lot of books!

School Day #176
Wednesday, June 15

Today we enjoyed watching the play *Really Rosie* performed by Mr. and Mrs. Pell's classes. It was particularly fun for us to watch the way they performed "A . . . Alligators All Around." We also watched a video about the summer reading program at the Cary and East Branch Libraries, which got us excited about visiting those libraries this summer for our summer books.

This marked the end of Ms. Yardley's communication to parents. She closed with a final thank you to parents for reading all the newsletters, responding to all the forms, contributing to the classroom parties, helping out on field trips, and participating in and supporting various projects. She acknowledged the countless invisible things she knew we had done at home to help make the year successful. Ms. Yardley commented on the children's hard work and enthusiasm, their good humor, and their love of learning.

Ms. Yardley's words were such a contrast to what Ted said one morning that week.

Wednesday, June 15

Dear Ted,

Today you spoke the words that parents dread even more than "That's boring": "I don't want to go to school today." I have no idea what precipitated your statement. Perhaps it was the restless night you had in 80-degree summerlike weather. Perhaps it was the report about "extremely silly behavior" we got from the staff in extended day yesterday, which required a talk. Perhaps you're just getting tired, as we all are, of the routine, the hectic pace, the anticipation of a school year ending. I think this could be your way of beginning to separate from kindergarten. We handled it, and you went to school and had a good day.

Love,

Mom

Sunday, June 19

Dear Ted,

Considering this is the last week of school, you seem collected and composed, happily ready for the year to draw to a close. Ms. Yardley has helped you and your class prepare for the transition to summer and then to first grade at summer's end. You keep reminding us that summer comes first and then first grade. What a good way to look at it.

Love,

Mom

THAnk YoU FoR YoUR HELP AND SUPPoRT!

Mary Yardley

TED

YoU ARE IMPoRTANT To US!

When I picked Ted up from extended day on the last Friday afternoon of the school year, he had many surprises for me—his backpack was bulging.

Friday, June 24

Dear Ted,

Today you brought home "some really great stuff," as you put it, in your backpack. Two irises peeked through the opening of your bag—a thank you to me from Ms. Yardley for the help I had given your class this year. When we arrived home we sat down and looked at all the stuff, and great it was.

There was a book called "An Important Book" about all the children in your class. It was a compilation of all the Important Books you had made this year for each person in your class. Your page was included right along with those of your friends.

What was different about this book was the personal letter from Ms. Yardley just to you. She said that she would always remember the wonderful boat you made with your dad from corks and toothpicks. She reminded you of how your idea gave the class the idea to make

I will always remember that wonderful boat you made with your dad and how the class made boats like yours and experimented and played with them in the water pool the last few weeks of school.
—Ms. Yardley

boats like yours and how much fun it was experimenting with them. I remember your taking the boat into school one day, cushioned with tissues in a small box. She closed by saying how much she would miss you, how she hoped you'd have a wonderful summer, and that she knew you would do well in first grade. You smiled as I read her words to you.

There was a second book called "My Kindergarten Self-Portraits," and the photograph you had brought in at the beginning of the year served as the cover. As you paged through you told me which self-portraits you especially liked and why. I noticed the smiles and saw something interesting to like in each.

There was your writing portfolio—a selection of writing samples dated from September to June.

There was a paper bagful of your artwork, which had decorated your classroom walls.

And there was a Certificate of Congratulations for the "wonderful work you did in kindergarten." What a good way to put it.

I, of course, couldn't prevent my eyes from misting as I read the personal full-page letter Ms. Yardley wrote to you. My mind flashed back to the letter you had received from Ms. Yardley at the end of last summer asking you to bring the photograph of yourself to share with the class. I remember being impressed at the time that your teacher had communicated personally with every child in the class. I end the year, however, even more amazed that during the crazy last days of school Ms. Yardley composed a personal letter to each child using words revealing her genuine connection with that child.

A few minutes later, as we were getting ready to go out for dinner, you said matter-of-factly, "Ms. Yardley is a great teacher, and I am going to miss her."

"So am I," I replied.

Love,

Mom

Epilogue

As I look back over the journal I kept during Ted's first year in school, I am struck by how emotion laden the process of parenting a child through school is. As a teacher I had definite opinions about what I considered to be an effective classroom environment and quality teaching. As a parent I had hopes for the kind of experience I wanted for my child. Throughout Ted's school career I'll probably struggle with this dual role. Sometimes it seemed I saw Ted and his school through my teacher eyes; other times I viewed events and experiences through my parent eyes. Neither perspective, of course, necessarily reflected Ted's viewpoint. Like many children—especially boys, I think—Ted was often reserved in his comments about what school was like for him, and I was left hungry for information about the increasing number of hours he spent away from home. Perhaps this is as it should and must be, but as a first-time parent I hadn't anticipated it.

I also didn't fully appreciate how a school year would be characterized by periods of ups and downs. While the bumps along the way can be anxiety producing for parents and children alike, they are also critical for growth. Children need opportunities to learn how to adjust to new people, routines, and expectations. They need to accept change as inevitable and develop confidence that they will indeed be able to grow into new situations and handle themselves competently and purposefully. While I do believe that most children are extraordinarily adaptable and resilient and can make the necessary adjustments during the course of a year, it is key for the adults in their lives to know how and when to assist them. For this reason I feel very strongly about the tremendous value of teacher communication.

Just as many new parents seek out other new parents for support, parents of school-age children long for that same kind of connection to help ease their transition to a new phase in the child's life. While this can be valuable and useful, it is no substitute for the kind of information and support that can be offered by a teacher who has a coherent, well-developed philosophy of education that really fits the needs of young children and who also sees it as her responsibility to articulate that philosophy in a manner accessible to parents.

Because Ms. Yardley shared with the parents her reasons for doing things and her philosophy of educating children, I developed trust, respect, and confidence in her. I knew she would provide for the needs not only of my child but of the community of children entrusted to her. Through her weekly communications she forged a partnership with me and every parent in her classroom who took the time to read her words. We could think about them and use them to help us pay closer attention to the ways in which our children were growing and developing as learners and as people.

I believe it will be important to keep an open mind each year about the different classroom environments and teaching styles my son will encounter during his public-school career. While I no doubt will have a higher comfort level with some teachers than with others, so too will Ted. My own confidence and trust in any teacher will depend on the teacher's communicating effectively and welcoming parents as partners.

Information about NAEYC

NAEYC is . . .

an organization of more than 101,000 members founded in 1926 and committed to fostering the growth and development of children from birth through age 8. Membership is open to all who share a desire to serve and act on behalf of the needs and rights of young children.

NAEYC provides . . .

educational services and resources to adults and programs working with and for children, including

• *Young Children, the* peer-reviewed journal for early childhood educators
• **Books, posters, brochures, and videos** to expand your knowledge and commitment to and support your work with young children and families, including topics on infants, curriculum, research, discipline, teacher education, and parent involvement

• An **Annual Conference** that brings people together from all over the United States and other countries to share their expertise and advocate on behalf of children and families

• **Week of the Young Child** celebrations sponsored by more than 400 NAEYC Affiliate Groups to call public attention to the critical significance of the child's early years

(continued)

- **Insurance plans** for members and programs

- **Public affairs** information and access to information through NAEYC resources and communication systems for conducting knowledgeable advocacy efforts at all levels of government and through the media

- **A voluntary accreditation system** for high-quality programs for children through the National Academy of Early Childhood Programs

- **Resources and services** through the National Institute for Early Childhood Professional Development, working to improve the quality and consistency of early childhood preparation and professional development opportunities

- **Young Children International** to promote international communication and information exchanges

For free information about membership, publications, or other NAEYC services, visit the **NAEYC Website** at **http://www.naeyc.org**

National Association for the Education of Young Children
1509 16th Street, NW, Washington, DC 20036-1426
202-232-8777 or 800-424-2460